W9-BUW-497

This Year of Our Lord

This Year of Our Lord

SERMONS FOR SPECIAL OCCASIONS

by

ANDREW WATTERSON BLACKWOOD

PHILADELPHIA

THE WESTMINSTER PRESS

COPYRIGHT, MCMXLIII, BY THE WESTMINSTER PRESS

All rights reserved — no part of this book may be reproduced in any form without permission in writing from the publisher, except by a reviewer who wishes to quote brief passages in connection with a review written for magazine or newspaper.

This book is manufactured in accord with orders issued by the War Production Board for conserving paper and other materials.

PRINTED IN THE UNITED STATES OF AMERICA

252.05
B 63t
C. 1.

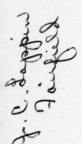

J. C. Sagan

gift

Sept. 1953

Dedicated to
the Mother of Our Sons,
Who Love to Preach and Sing

18650

FOREWORD

EVERY parish ought to have days that glow on the calendar of life. The best of them should come from the Church Year, as a legacy richer than gold. For example, think of Christmas, Easter, and Pentecost. When the hour of worship includes a message about Christ, or the heavenly Father, the minister ought to rejoice. But he should likewise sense the need of sermons about the human side of our religion. Such preaching calls for the interpretation of life today, in light that comes from God through the man in the pulpit.

Sermons for red-letter occasions are difficult to prepare. Among all the messages of the year these may prove the most troublesome, if not the least helpful. A clergyman of a certain type, not common of late, drags into the pulpit what belongs out on the street. A man of another sort, not so unusual, fails to show the bearing of divine truth on human needs today. According to Frederick D. Maurice, a minister can be of little use to his generation unless he devotes himself mainly to the problems of his time.

My purpose, then, is to show the will of God for busy folk in a world that has been at war, and during years of reconstruction. Since the aim is practical, the style should be simple. With one or two exceptions the sermons are new in form. A number of the texts carry over from other days. Many of the leading ideas have long been my friends. But few of the words had appeared on paper twelve months ago. In view of current needs and hopes, the treatment concerns today, as well as tomorrow.

The book is a labor of love. The one to whom it is dedicated has been asking me to put some of my sermons into durable shape. Recently the editor responsible for my work on *The Funeral* has persuaded me to prepare this volume. However, I alone have marked out the field. I include more special sermons than if I were a pastor. One reason is that I have in view no single flock. A book of another sort would need a golden cord to bind all the parts in one. But messages for red-letter days ought to differ as much as stars in the sky.

Well do I recall the gibe of James M. Barrie. He says that something unwelcome seems " as solemn as a volume of sermons printed by request! " If Sir James had ever toiled as a pastor, visiting the sick and comforting the dying, and then had stood in the pulpit on the Lord's Day, looking into the faces of friends who filled all the pews, he would not have said " solemn." Why not " helpful "?

My aim throughout is to prove helpful. At heart I am a pastor. I also love to preach. In the pulpit I feel more highly favored than anyone else on earth, except a brother minister. In the study much the same spirit prevails. Hence I have enjoyed preparing these messages. As the book goes forth, may the Spirit of God shine upon my written words and bring the truth to light in the face of the Redeemer.

ANDREW WATTERSON BLACKWOOD.

THE THEOLOGICAL SEMINARY
PRINCETON, NEW JERSEY.

ACKNOWLEDGMENTS

The author is grateful to the following for permission to quote from books subject to copyright:

American Tract Society: Four poems from *Bees in Amber*, by John Oxenham.

Doubleday, Doran & Co., Inc.: Excerpts from "Roofs," in *Main Street and Other Poems*, by Joyce Kilmer; *The Story of My Life*, by Helen Keller.

E. P. Dutton & Co., Inc.: Excerpt from *Man and Society in Calamity*, by Pitirim A. Sorokin.

Farrington, Mrs. Dora Davis: "The Harvard Prize Hymn," by Harry W. Farrington.

Freeman, Mrs. Margery: A poem by Robert Freeman.

Harper & Brothers: Excerpt from "Indifference," in *The Sorrows of God*, by G. A. Studdert-Kennedy.

Houghton Mifflin Company: Excerpt from " To Harvard College," in *School, College, and Character*, by L. B. R. Briggs; excerpt from "The Eternal Goodness," by J. G. Whittier.

The Macmillan Company: Excerpts from "The Everlasting Mercy" and "The Seekers," in *Poems*, by John Masefield; *Poetical Works*, by Christina Rossetti; *Memoirs of My Childhood and Youth*, by Albert Schweitzer; "Maud," in *Poems*, by Alfred Tennyson; and *The Day Must Dawn*, by Alice Sligh Turnbull.

Markham, Virgil: Two poems by Edwin Markham.

Charles Scribner's Sons: Excerpts from "The Crystal," in *Poems*, by Sidney Lanier; "The Builders," in *The Poems of Henry Van Dyke*.

Many of the Biblical quotations are from the King James Version, because of its rhythm. Some are from the

American Standard Version, for the sake of accuracy. Occasionally the rendering is from the original language. In a few places I am indebted to the recent translations, especially the one by Dr. James Moffatt, and that by Drs. Smith and Goodspeed.

CONTENTS

"What hath this day deserv'd?   What hath it done,
That it in golden letters should be set
Among the high tides in the calendar?"

— KING JOHN, ACT III, SCENE 1

THE COMFORT IN HANDEL'S MESSIAH

*" Comfort ye, comfort ye my people, saith your
God. Speak home to the heart of Jerusalem." —
Isa. 40:1 (Hebrew) .*

THESE words from the prophet sound the keynote of
Handel's *Messiah*. Like many another golden passage
in the Bible, our text came out of dark days. After a
succession of wars and kindred calamities, God's people
had been carried into captivity. In exile they faced all
the problems of reconstruction. Hence their souls were
full of dire forebodings. With broken hearts and blasted
hopes, what did they need so much as comfort?

Handel's *Messiah,* also, came out of dark and troublous days. During the latter part of 1741, when he composed the oratorio at Dublin, the hearts of the Irish people were filled with unrest and fears. Early in 1743, when
the music was first rendered in London, the English people appeared to be ready for revolution. In that year
Charles Wesley seems to have written " Hymns for Times
of Trouble." By the providence of God, largely through
the Wesleyan movement, England escaped revolution.
While the Methodist Revival was getting under way,
hosts of brokenhearted folk in Britain must have found
comfort in Handel's oratorio.

Both in our text and in *The Messiah* everything re-
volves round the idea of comfort. Since that serves as the
motif of the present discourse, we ought to remind ourselves what comfort means. To comfort is to strengthen
the heart through looking to God. For most of us today, as

for Jerusalem of old, the times call for strengthening the
soul, not for weeping on the shoulder; for lifting up the
heart, not for laying down the burden; for engaging in
Christian service, not for indulging in self-pity.

In short, we should come close to the heart of God, and
not think so much about ourselves. From this point of
view, let us now give heed to the text. It strikes the keynote of Handel's *Messiah*. There we can find comfort
amid a war-swept world. " Comfort ye, comfort ye my
people, saith your God. Speak home to the heart of
Jerusalem."

1. *The Comfort in Handel's* Messiah *Attracts the
Hearts of God's People.* " Speak home to the heart of
Jerusalem." To us the word Jerusalem means the
dwelling place of God's children. Especially in days of
distress our religion should often speak to the broken
of heart. In Handel's day, says a student of English history, " those who cared for religion and morality had
forgotten that man is an imaginative and emotional being." On our side of the water, at the time when Handel was composing his oratorio, Jonathan Edwards
was preaching a series of sermons that later appeared
in a book, *A Treatise Concerning Religious Affections.*
There he shows that " true religion, in a great part, consists in the affections. . . . The Author of human nature
has not only given the affections to men, but has made
them very much the springs of action."

If we in the Church would appeal to a war-swept
world we must form the habit of speaking more often to
the heart. We are dealing with " truths that never can
be proved." But they can be known by the heart. We
serve amid a world twice blasted by " total war." We

know that " there are worse things than war, and that war is the cause of them every one." For living examples of war's aftermath, we may turn to our own history. Between 1865 and 1876 some of our Southern states suffered under so-called " Reconstruction." Or else we can look across to Europe. What have innocent peoples there not endured since Armistice Day in 1918? Behold what war hath wrought! Is it any wonder that the hearts of men and women everywhere cry out for comfort? In China and elsewhere multitudes of little boys and girls have become broken in heart and maimed in body.

Give heed then to Isaiah. In the name of his God, the prophet is speaking to a city that has often been besieged. " Her warfare is accomplished." Thank God for that! But listen once more: " She hath received of the Lord's hand double for all her sins." So it appears that the roots of war lie hidden in hearts infested with sin. Amid all the wrongs that have led the world to war, we at home have had our share. As a witness hear the Apostle James: " Whence come wars and fightings among you? come they not hence, even of your lusts? " Never do our sins appear more ghastly than when we view them in the light of their aftereffects. If we are to receive comfort, therefore, we must have a Gospel that brings pardon, cleansing, and peace.

Today all over the world the choice seems to rest between a religion of comfort and hope and an experience of chaos and despair. In 1941 a wise student of world history, Pitirim A. Sorokin, of Harvard, sent forth a book on *The Crisis of Our Age.* There he showed that our world has come to the end of the present order, and that all the nations stand at the parting of the ways. His more recent work, *Man and Society in Calamity,* paints a dreadful picture of the depths to which our so-called civilization has sunk. Nevertheless, he bids us lift up our hearts. Through the Gospel of the Kingdom, he assures us, we can work our way out of the present crisis. But "without the Kingdom," he insists, "we are doomed to a weary and torturing pilgrimage from calamity to calamity, from crisis to crisis, with only brief moments of improvement for regaining our breath."

Dr. E. Stanley Jones also stresses the supremacy of the Kingdom. To such an appeal for putting first the Kingdom of God, many a practical man turns a deaf ear. "All that may be well enough for university professors and missionaries," he declares, "but do make clear what religion means to a man like me!" That request sounds fair. For the answer we turn again to our text. It reminds us that religion concerns the heart more than the head, and that the heart finds comfort in God the Father.

Much the same truth rings out from Whittier's poem, "The Eternal Goodness," which he gave to the world in 1865, the closing year of the War Between the States. As one of the common people and a lover of peace, the Quaker poet found comfort only in his religion. Once he wrote to a friend: "We cannot get along without God, and of Him we are sure."

> " I see the wrong that round me lies,
>   I feel the guilt within;
> I hear, with groans and travail-cries,
>   The world confess its sin.

> " Yet in the maddening maze of things,
>   And tossed by storm and flood,
> To one fixed trust my spirit clings;
>   I know that God is good! "

2. *The Comfort in* The Messiah *Flows from the Heart of God*. In the Christian religion, as in all of life, everything good comes from God. In the New Testament, as in the Old, practically every golden text about salvation begins with God the Father. Oftentimes he talks to his children in personal pronouns. As Martin Luther says, the glory of our religion appears in its use of pronouns. Among the threescore and ten golden texts in *The Messiah*, more than half show our God speaking with such intimate pronouns as those of the text: " Comfort ye my people. . . . Behold your God! "

What satisfaction we ought to derive from those two words: " My people "! Unworthy as we are, much as we deserve to suffer, still we belong to God. Later in the chapter we learn that he never faints or ceases to strengthen his children. Let us therefore praise God for his perseverance. " Even the youths shall faint and be weary, and the young men shall utterly fall: But they that wait upon the Lord shall renew their strength." To wait upon him calls for " the trust of weakness in strength." " The weakness that waits upon God soon becomes strong. "

Assurance likewise streams from those other words: " Behold your God! " According to A. B. Davidson, wise man of Edinburgh, the Old Testament contains but a single message: God. The comfort flows from his willingness to call us children. When we acquaint ourselves with him we can be at peace. Of course we can never understand his ways of dealing with the world or with ourselves as his children. But through faith and love we can seek in him " our Shelter from the stormy blast, and our eternal Home."

Through trust in God one finds abundant reason for

hope. " Why art thou cast down, O my soul? and why art thou disquieted within me? hope in God: for I shall yet praise him, who is the health of my countenance, and my God." Thus did the psalmist learn to rely upon God when there could be no other refuge. If anyone asks how he can receive such comfort today, again the reply comes from Handel's masterpiece.

3. *The Comfort in* The Messiah *Centers in the Son of God.* At the beginning and at the end, the oratorio sings about the Father. But as a whole *The Messiah* sounds forth the praises of the Son. The first main part shows how God comforts his children through the Advent of the Redeemer. The second part tells how God comforts his people through the cross. The last part reveals God's comfort for us all through the Kingship of Christ. From beginning to end, *The Messiah* sounds the glories of the incarnate Lord as Redeemer and King.

In keeping with the order of the main parts in *The Messiah,* let us first look on Christ as King. What comfort we should enjoy if only we took our stand on " the crown rights of the Redeemer "! Surely our war-blasted world needs such a Ruler! In 1922, Benito Mussolini stole the scepter of Italy. Instead of an apology, he said, with a sneer, that he had seen the throne rooms of Europe standing empty and that he had moved into the one he coveted most. After twenty-one years as an overlord, he was forced to give up his ill-gotten glory. In view of such facts, is it not time for the nations to seek their security in Christ as King? Who but he can bring peace on earth, good will toward men? That may be why Tennyson sings in " Maud ":

" Put down the passions that make earth hell!
Down with ambition, avarice, pride,
Jealousy, down! cut off from the mind
The bitter springs of anger and fear!
Down too, down at your own fireside,
With the evil tongue and the evil ear,
For each is at war with mankind! "

The oratorio likewise presents our Lord as the Good
Shepherd: " He shall feed his flock like a shepherd, and
he shall gather the lambs with his arm." Here the stress
falls on his gentleness. Who but Jesus can be so gracious
and kind, so long-suffering towards the weak and the
helpless? Thus he appears in the most beloved of all the
psalms: " The Lord is my shepherd; I shall not want."
Above all does he wish to shield and bless the little children, one by one:

" A Shepherd He with gentle charms;
A lamb I see within His arms."

The Gospel in *The Messiah* never moves the heart
more strongly than when one hears about the " Love
Divine, that stooped to share our sharpest pang, our
bitterest tear." In the Gospels one fourth of the space
is devoted to scenes near the cross; in Handel's masterpiece two fifths of the music concerns the death of the
Redeemer. This central part of the oratorio begins with
the call of John, the evangelist to the common people:
" Behold the Lamb of God, that taketh away the sins of
the world." Gradually the music leads up to the " Hallelujah Chorus ": " King of kings! and Lord of lords!
Hallelujah! " After that the third main part must be
short. Otherwise there would be anticlimax.

Thus far we have looked at the comfort in *The Messiah* from three points of view. This comfort attracts the

hearts of God's people, flows from the heart of the Father himself, and centers in the heart of Christ. Hence we ought to sing: " Praise God from whom all blessings flow "! But perhaps some practical friend has one more request: " Pray tell me where I can find this comfort today." The answer is not far to seek: Look for words of comfort where Handel found them, in the Holy Scriptures.

4. *The Comfort in* The Messiah *Is Embodied in the Book.* " How firm a foundation, ye saints of the Lord, is laid for your faith in His excellent Word!" Where but in the Bible could Handel have found such an array of consoling truths? According to one way of figuring, *The Messiah* contains seventy-two verses. Of that number, two thirds come from the Old Testament. In the group as a whole the discerning spirit can find the peace of God, which passeth all understanding. What a message for this Advent season!

When we look to the Scriptures for words of comfort, why not let Handel serve as our guide? He knows how to choose golden texts! He asks us to start with the fortieth chapter of Isaiah and then move on through that mountain country of the Old Testament. At times we may not understand what the prophet means. Nevertheless, everywhere in the latter part of Isaiah we can behold the goodness of our God.

The author of *The Messiah* would also have us saturate our souls in some of the psalms. Here he singles out certain songs that have to do with sufferings undeserved, but borne with patience from above. Once again, the value of the reading depends on the willing heart, not on the well-stocked brain. Whenever one turns to

The Book of Psalms in quest of comfort and peace, one ought to behold dim foreshadowings of the cross.

In the New Testament our mentor begins with The Gospel According to St. Luke. In " the most beautiful book ever written," Handel discovers the grace of Jesus Christ. That means in part His love and saving help for the weakest and worst of mankind. From Luke the oratorio leads us gradually to the Resurrection Chapter written by the Apostle Paul.

Erelong our guide takes us into The Revelation of St. John the Divine. There we may find it hard to keep our footing. But if we let our hearts have their way, we shall quickly learn that God is able to sanctify our deepest distress. Hence *The Messiah* closes with a triumphant ascription of praise to God the Father: "Blessing and honor, glory and pow'r be unto him, . . . that sitteth upon the throne, and unto the Lamb for ever and ever. . . . Amen."

If all this reading would take too much time, single out the seventy-two verses that form the basis of *The Messiah*. These golden texts appear in clusters. They comprise only about thirty passages, each of them short. In fact, *The Messiah* as a whole is little more than half as long as the Sermon on the Mount. You can read the entire text of the oratorio in a very few minutes. You will find it more interesting and helpful, however, if you move somewhat slowly.

For instance, note the quality of the voice to which the composer assigns a certain solo. Ask yourself why it should be the tenor, and not the contralto, to whom he gives the opening words: " Comfort ye, comfort ye my people, saith your God." Above all, give heed to the tone color of the choruses, beginning with this one: " The glory of the Lord shall be revealed, and all flesh shall see it together; for the mouth of the Lord hath spoken it."

Between now and Christmas, why not make a loving study of all these words? Why not commit them to memory and thus prepare to use them in helping others who stand in need of comfort? If you live with these golden texts day after day, perhaps for only a few minutes at a time, you will discover in God the Source of all comfort. You will also find that you are walking in pathways of peace. Thus you will come closer and closer still to the God of all comfort and grace.

The Golden Texts in The Messiah

As an aid in reading during the Advent season, I give here a list of the texts that appear in Handel's *Messiah*. Since the third main part is short, I have stretched it out to fill up the space. If anyone wishes to use these facts in a Church bulletin, or elsewhere, he is as free as the sunshine. The edition is that of T. Tertius Noble, revised by Max Spicker, according to Handel's original score, and printed by G. Schirmer, Inc., New York, 1912.

Part One	*Part Two*	*Part Three*
Isaiah 40:1, 2, 3	John 1:29	Job 19:25
Isaiah 40:4, 5	Isaiah 53:3	Job 19:26
Haggai 2:6, 7	Isaiah 50:6	I Corinthians 15:20
Malachi 3:1, 2, 3	Isaiah 53:4, 5, 6	I Corinthians 15:21
Isaiah 7:14	Psalm 22:7, 8	I Corinthians 15:22
Isaiah 40:9	Psalm 69:20	I Corinthians 15:51
Isaiah 60:2, 3	Lamentations 1:12	I Corinthians 15:52
Isaiah 9:2	Isaiah 53:8	I Corinthians 15:53
Isaiah 9:6	Psalm 16:10	I Corinthians 15:54
	Psalm 24:7, 8, 10	I Corinthians 15:55
Luke 2:8, 9	Hebrews 1:5, 6	I Corinthians 15:56
Luke 2:10, 11	Psalm 68:18, 11	I Corinthians 15:57
Luke 2:13, 14	Isaiah 52:7	Romans 8:31
Zechariah 9:9, 10	Psalm 19:4	Romans 8:33
Isaiah 35:5, 6	Psalm 2:1, 2, 3, 4, 9	Romans 8:34
Isaiah 40:11	Revelation 19:6	
Matthew 11:28, 29	Revelation 11:15	Revelation 5:12
Matthew 11:30	Revelation 19:16	Revelation 5:13

THE BACKGROUND OF CHRISTMAS
*" The Word became flesh, and tented among us,
and we beheld his glory." — John 1:14 (Greek)* .

CHRISTMAS DAY will glow all the more brightly if
we remember what it means. Lying beneath its beauty,
in the midst of our merriment, we should behold the
wonder of the Gospel. From the very morning of life we
have known that " Gospel " means Good News from
the Father God to the children of men. At a time when
our sons have been engaged in countless battles, and vast
stretches of scorched earth cry out for replanting, many
of us feel the need of Good News. From the vision of
ruined cities and new-made graves we now turn aside to
listen while the angels sing about peace on earth, good
will toward men.

Meanwhile we ask, " What truth lies back of the
Christmas Gospel?" There can be only one reply: " The
Incarnation!" The word comes from the Latin, which
means " in the flesh." According to the latest and
most majestic of the Gospels, the Son of the Most
High took up his abode in human flesh, and lived
among us as in a tent. Looking back over the fleeting
years that commenced in Bethlehem, the Apostle John
could see the splendor of God shining out from that
tabernacle where for a generation the Lord Jesus found
his earthly abode.

Let us therefore think about the Incarnation, from
two contrasting points of view: The one has to do with

what it means in Christian thinking; the other concerns its bearing on Christian experience. Both the thinking and the experience should blend into one, much as light and heat issue from the same morning sun. In terms of beauty and warmth we should behold the background of Christmas Day. For that background the Gospel word is glory. " We beheld his glory," as from God.

1. *The Meaning of the Incarnation.* This truth lies at the background of all that Christians know about the earthly career of our Lord. The fact of the Incarnation appears among the deepest of the mysteries that cluster round the earthly life of the Redeemer. Amid all those mysteries, one reality shines out at the yuletide with a glory brighter than the Christmas star: the truth that the Child of Bethlehem came from above, and that he was divine.

" The Word became flesh." The " Word " is God's way of revealing himself to the children of men. In early times he made himself known through the prophets, who spoke and sang as they were moved by the Holy Spirit. In later years he brought fuller light through the apostles, who spoke and wrote about God in terms of Jesus Christ. To this very hour the Heavenly Father is revealing himself through the Bible, as well as through preaching. All the while his supreme method of making himself known has been through " the heaven-drawn picture of Christ, the living Word."

" We beheld his glory, the glory as of the only begotten of the Father." Glory means the outshining of the indwelling Light that we know as God. How the Most High could take up his abode in the heart of a little Babe, and dwell in the life of a growing Boy, eternity alone can

make clear. How the attractive goodness of the heavenly
Father could shine out through the Man of Galilee, and
supremely through the Christ of the cross, must ever remain a mystery. But the mystery is full of light, not of
darkness. Since we mortals insist on giving everything
holy a non-Biblical name, many of the fathers spoke of
the mystery as " the divinity of Christ." Some of us now
prefer to say " the deity of our Lord." But why quibble
about words?

This truth about the Redeemer as divine stands at
the heart of the Nicene Creed: " I believe . . . in one
Lord Jesus Christ, the only-begotten Son of God; Begotten of his Father before all worlds, God of God, Light
of Light, Very God of very God; Begotten, not made;
Being of one substance with the Father; By whom all
things were made: Who for us men and for our salvation
came down from heaven, And was incarnate by the Holy
Ghost of the Virgin Mary, And was made man: And was
crucified also for us under Pontius Pilate; He suffered
and was buried: And the third day he rose again according to the Scriptures: And ascended into heaven, And
sitteth on the right hand of the Father: And he shall
come again, with glory, to judge both the quick and the
dead; Whose kingdom shall have no end."

The mystery that clusters round Christmas grows
deeper when we remember that the Son of God was human as well as divine. In truth, according to Henry van
Dyke, and other reverent thinkers, Jesus dwelt among
men as " the human life of God." At Bethlehem the
Wise Men knelt down before a real baby. In the Temple
at Jerusalem twelve years later the " doctors " talked
with a real boy. Like every normal child in our com-

munity today, Jesus " increased in wisdom and stature, and in favour with God and man."

In the fullness of the years the Christ of Galilee became a man. His humanity was as real as his divinity. In fact, the human nature was far easier for men to see than the divine. In the carpenter shop of Nazareth, and throughout the busy years that led to the cross, Jesus toiled and suffered as a man. Hence the Roman judge spoke more wisely than he knew when he declared, " Behold the man! " Unfortunately, sacred art has failed to portray the strength and the vigor of Jesus' ideal manhood. For that reason many of us love to think of him as resembling young Seth, in George Eliot's moving tale, *Adam Bede*. Like his older brother, Seth was a giant. In his work as a carpenter and in his life at home, Seth Bede displayed much of the prowess and the gentleness that we behold in Jesus the man.

The mystery lying back of Christmas grows deeper still when we think of our Lord in terms of today. At Christmas time, and throughout the period leading up to Easter, we should look upon Christ as our Contemporary. How then shall we regard him, as human or divine? We find it hard to conceive of a perfect union between the noblest in heaven and the best on earth. Hence we persist in saying " either-or." " Either he is human or else he is divine." Throughout the Middle Ages, and in the Roman Church to this very hour, the stress has been on his deity. Among Protestants the emphasis has shifted to his humanity. In fact, for a while certain believing men adopted as their slogan, " Back to Jesus!" As though he were not living now, and with us here, even at Christmas time!

"Is Christ divided?" Should one segment of the Church believe only in the Jesus of the Sermon on the Mount, born at Bethlehem and dying on the cross, ever "meek and mild," but only as the best of men? Should another part of the Church revere him solely as the Christ of the creeds, high and lifted up, dwelling far above the prosaic level where we mortals live and work? Surely there can be only one Christ! Everywhere in the New Testament he appears both as human and divine. The human aspect of his being is as real and almost as precious as the divine. In Christ, and in him alone, "mercy and truth are met together; righteousness and peace have kissed each other."

In all these matters of Christian belief, "it is the heart, and not the brain, that to the highest doth attain." Whatever our questionings may be at other seasons of the year, our hearts should have their way at Christmas time. Let us kneel with the shepherds before the Babe of Bethlehem, and then listen to the angelic chorus about the Son of God. Thus our hearts tell us that in some way passing knowledge the Lord of Glory must be both human and divine. Hence we rejoice in the saying of Sir Edward Burne-Jones, the English painter. Late in life he was asked if he still accepted the Christmas story. That lover of sacred art replied, "It is too beautiful not to be true!"

The Christmas Gospel shows a perfect blending of the human and the divine. For this truth in some of its upper reaches we turn to the hymnal, where the noblest of the yuletide songs appeal to the heart. In a city of the Middle West two groups of ministers and laymen once used up their energies through more than a year in quarreling about whether the Lord Jesus was divine or human. At Christmas time more than two thousand little boys and girls assembled in the city auditorium, and with gladness of heart sang together the most beautiful of the old-time carols. At the end of an hour radiant with the spirit of heaven on earth, a mother sitting up in the balcony said with a sigh of relief, " As long as we can sing the yuletide hymns we shall never lose the Christmas Gospel." In much the same spirit Harry W. Farrington writes:

> " I know not how that Bethelem's Babe
>   Could in the Godhead be;
>   I only know the Manger Child
>   Has brought God's life to me.
>
> " I know not how that Calvary's cross
>   A world from sin could free;
>   I only know its matchless love
>   Has brought God's love to me."

2. *The Spirit of the Incarnation.* At Christmas time, many of us need to discover afresh that the Incarnation has everything to do with Christian experience. Otherwise we may content ourselves with sitting up in the balcony and looking down on our little children as they joyfully acclaim the Christ of Christmas. Rather should we join with the Magi in their quest of Him who alone can be the Light of the world. " Wise Men still worship." Why not kneel with them now as they present their gifts of gold, frankincense, and myrrh? Just as the Lord Jesus is both human and divine, so is the Incarnation both an assured fact of Christian belief and a blessed reality in Christian experience.

The Incarnation shows " the meaning of God in human experience." As little boys, some of us were obliged to learn a famous definition: " God is a Spirit, infinite, eternal, and unchangeable, in his being, wisdom, power, holiness, justice, goodness, and truth." Today we accept that statement word for word, but only with our minds. In fact, we think of all that frozen splendor in terms of " Greenland's icy mountains." But when by faith we enter into the spirit of the Incarnation we find that God is here with us now, he cares for us mortals, and he is able to do for us far more than our hearts can desire:

> " God is Love; His mercy brightens
> All the path in which we rove;
> Bliss He wakes, and woe He lightens:
> God is Wisdom; God is Love."

Thus the Incarnation reveals the best truths we can know about God as our Father. Never has he lived as an infinite absentee. Surely he makes his home in the heavens, and he must ever be far above our thoughts of him. But the Father God likewise yearns to dwell in our hearts and our homes. Through what he did for us all at Christmas time, and still more on Calvary, we learn how " nigh is grandeur to our dust," how " near is God to man." Hence we ought to exclaim with the Apostle Paul, " If God be for us, who can be against us? "

The Incarnation also makes clear and luminous the most wonderful truth about man. In the fact of Christ's coming we learn that the heart of a man is able to receive the indwelling God. Hence we should look upon every little baby as like the One born at Bethlehem, and every growing boy or girl as resembling Jesus of Nazareth. That is the ideal. For a lad or a lass twelve years of age, being a Christian ought to mean becoming like Christ when he was that age and that size. May the beauty of the Lord our God rest upon our sons and daughters, as well as our children's children! In the wonder of life's morning let each of them become like the Lord Jesus. Throughout the circling years may they one and all prove loyal to the " strong Son of God, immortal Love "!

The Incarnation likewise shows the meaning of the Christian life. When the Son of God veiled his glory to dwell in human flesh, he gave us a perfect example of what it means to live on earth as a child of the Heavenly Father. Through the Incarnation, Jesus also brought us the motive power by which we can become worthy to be called sons and daughters of the Living God. For instance, when the Apostle Paul was pleading with his friends at Corinth to be generous in their giving, he held up as an ideal the Incarnation: " Ye know the grace of our Lord Jesus Christ, that, though he was rich, yet for your sakes he became poor, that ye through his poverty might be rich."

Once again, the apostle bids us take the Incarnation as the pattern for all our Christian living: " Let this mind be in you, which was also in Christ Jesus." " The mind of the Master " was Christ's way of looking out upon the world. For him life on earth meant a call to humble himself, an opportunity to serve his fellow men, and a need to make the supreme sacrifice. To be a Christian now must mean to be like him in spirit and in truth. If anyone ever begins to feel proud and self-sufficient, even selfish and grasping, holding back from the summons of God for the giving up of self, let him remember the spirit that brought the Redeemer from heaven to earth. Being a Christian means to " live a manly life for Jesus' sake, and a godly life for humanity's sake."

So mysterious and so sublime is the truth of the In-

carnation that words must fail one who tries to show its
bearing on human experience today. Fortunately, however, some of God's children have displayed more than
a little of the spirit that brought the Lord to earth at
Christmas time. For example, in 1913, Thomas Mott
Osborne became chairman of the New York State Com-
mission for Prison Reform. Before he entered upon his
active duties, he arranged to be incarcerated for a week
at Auburn State Prison. There he was known simply as
Tom Brown. He lived in a cell — or at least he existed
— and endured for a time the privations of a typical
convict. By the fellowship of those sufferings the future
warden of Sing Sing Prison learned much that he needed
to know in order to befriend the convicts and thus help
them to reform.

A chaplain who served at the time in Auburn Prison
vouches for the facts that follow. Into the cell where
" Tom Brown " had been confined there came a hardened criminal. When he learned what the other man
had done, and why, the convict's heart was touched by
that living example of unselfishness and sacrifice.
Through the ministrations of the chaplain, the criminal
gave his heart to Christ and became a model prisoner,
as well as a personal worker. On the human level he owed
his salvation to " Tom Brown." Would that there might
be such a change in every wrongdoer as he draws near to
Christmas Day! " If any man be in Christ, he is a new
creature: old things are passed away; behold, all things
are become new."

Fortunately, one need not be a hardened convict in
order to take part in bidding Christ welcome. Those
who hail him most gladly may be little boys and girls.
In the spirit of love and trust open up your heart to him

now. Let him come in as Saviour and King. " But as many as received him, to them gave he power to become the sons of God, even to them that believe on his name." If such is your experience today, you will see the wonder that lies in the background of Christmas: " The Word became flesh, and tented among us, and we beheld his glory."

Heavenly Father, at this glad Christmas time show us how rich we are in Christ, and how poor we should be without him. Through thy Spirit enable each of us to become like him in the riches of his love and mercy, for our prayer is in his name. Amen.

NEW YEAR'S SUNDAY
Matt. 6:19–34

THE TEXT FOR THE NEW YEAR
*" Thy kingdom come. Thy will be done in earth,
as it is in heaven." — Matt. 6:10.*

THESE words suggest a motto for coming days. On this
closing Sunday of the year many laymen wish the minister to preach from a golden text that will serve them as a
guiding star throughout the ensuing months. In the
midst of change and chaos we all need something high
and fixed. In a world that has been at war those who love
the Lord should be able to steer by the stars and not by
the waves.

As a motto for the New Year, what could prove more
fitting than the words of our text? They appear in the
Sermon on the Mount. There they lie at the heart of the
Lord's Prayer. " Thy kingdom come "! What could be
simpler or more sublime? When rightly understood,
these words give the substance of the Christian religion
and life. However, through constant use they have become so familiar that sometimes they seem commonplace. If we are to restore their pristine luster, we must
remember what they mean.

As if in response to our unspoken question the Master
explains this portion of the Lord's Prayer. " Thy kingdom come " means " Thy will be done in earth, as it is in
heaven." The Kingdom of God, therefore, points to the
realm in which his people do his holy will. Ideally, the
petition makes us think of heaven. There everyone does
the will of the Heavenly Father. That is the Kingdom of

God in glory. But the Lord's Prayer has to do chiefly with mortals here below. It concerns the way we ought to live here and now: " Thy will be done in earth." This truth may seem more real if we paraphrase the words as follows: " Thy will be done in our community today, as it is done in the city of God evermore." Such modern diction makes us thank God anew for the simplicity of the Master: " Thy kingdom come. Thy will be done in earth, as it is in heaven."

The words suggest three lines of thought about the Kingdom of God in our midst today. The first is the most vital. Hence that is where we take our start.

1. *The Kingdom Is Divine.* This truth may sound simple. Nevertheless, it sums up all we know about religion and life. The Kingdom is divine. It is the Kingdom of God. Someone may protest: " The Heavenly Father has given the authority to Christ as our King." That is true, most gloriously. But surely our Lord has taught us to look on the Kingdom as belonging to God the Father Almighty: " Seek ye first the kingdom of God."

In the phrase " the kingdom of God " the stress falls on the word at the end. God founded the Kingdom of old. He watches over it now. He guarantees that it will endure forever. Even in the darkest hours of earth he can depend on a host of his servants to be loyal unto death. At the close of the present age his cause will triumph. " The kingdoms of this world are become the kingdoms of our Lord, and of his Christ." Then the Prince of Glory shall reign over the earth he died to redeem. How do we know? " We have Christ's own promise, and that cannot fail."

The coming of God's Kingdom depends chiefly on him, not on us. That is why we pray, " Thy kingdom come." He who has begun a good work in the world will not cease until that work is finished. Back of his Kingdom on earth stand the wisdom and the power, as well as the boundless resources, of the Triune God. It makes a vast deal of difference to us mortals that we serve the God who perseveres. Whenever we do his will on earth we fall in line with the loftiest and the noblest movements in all the world. Other causes that once seemed mighty as Gibraltar have crumbled, but the Kingdom of God shall endure. Whatever reverses the coming year may bring to the forces of truth and honor, those who keep doing the will of God day after day can rest secure. The Kingdom must triumph. Back of it stands Eternal God.

In things temporal as well as spiritual it is good to enjoy a sense of security. It is heartening to know that one's investments for home and loved ones are safe. Throughout the land in 1933 banks large and small were forced to close their doors. In more recent years failures of that sort have become rare. When such an institution goes on the rocks, the depositors need not suffer loss. Back of every bank in our country stands the Government of the United States. Hence there should be a sense of security about such investments. In fact, we accept the guarantee of bank deposits as a matter of course.

In a far loftier realm why not employ the same principle? Even if our Government should someday go down, the Word of our God would endure. The feeling of security about things spiritual depends on the fact that God stands back of his Kingdom. As his beloved children we are laying up treasures in heaven by doing his will on earth. We can trust him to safeguard those treasures for time and eternity. In brief, here is the best thing we mortals can know about the Kingdom: It belongs to God. It is divine. Such a message comes through the poem by Richard C. Trench, " The Kingdom of God ":

> " I say to thee, do thou repeat
> To the first man thou mayest meet
> In lane, highway, or open street —

> " That he and we and all men move
> Under a canopy of love,
> As broad as the blue sky above."

2. *The Kingdom Is Human.* The words " Thy kingdom come " mean " Thy will be done in earth." In other words, the Kingdom is human. In its source and in its power the Kingdom must ever be as divine as God himself. It is the realm where he lives and moves and has his being. But from our point of view the Kingdom must also be human. If it were vocal it might exclaim, " Nothing human is foreign to me! " To God's children here below, life should prove simple at heart. Being Christians ought to mean doing the will of our Heavenly Father. In so far as we mortals can tell, this world is the only part of God's universe where the will of our God is not being done. Is it any wonder then that we mortals pray: " Thy kingdom come "?

The Kingdom comes, as a rule, to one person at a time. Sooner or later every one of us must face the question, Am I living to do the will of God, or am I trying to go my own gait? Surely the best time to become a Christian and start doing the will of God is in the beauty of life's morning. Would that every growing boy or girl in our community might be a Christian today. By a Christian one means being like Jesus when he was that age and that size. Then it would not be long before we should begin to remake our part of the world. That is why Horace Bushnell's classic book, *Christian Nurture*, contains a chapter on " The Out-Populating Power of the Christian Stock." He means that the ideal way to advance the Kingdom of God on earth is to win the boys and girls, one by one.

If not in childhood, then the time to become a follower of Christ is before one crosses the threshold into manhood or womanhood. Among all the vital choices that confront any youth or maiden, the most momentous is this: Whom shall I serve, God or myself? Shall I make it my chief concern to do the will of the Heavenly Father, or shall I insist on having my own way? " It is said that when Aaron Burr reached the age of twenty-one he faced this issue squarely. Deliberately he resolved to turn his back on the God of his fathers. Doubtless for this reason one of the most brilliant men in American history made a shipwreck of his life. Today at Princeton Cemetery his bones lie buried at the foot of his grandfather's grave. Those two, Jonathan Edwards and Aaron Burr, illustrate the difference between the man who seeks first the Kingdom of God and the one who chooses slavery to self.

If not in childhood or youth, the time to start doing the will of God is in mature manhood, or even old age. Whatever a person's years, the hour to get right with God is the one now ready to strike on the clock. In the Scriptures the majority of the conversions recorded took place after youth had fled. Now that hosts of men and women have become disillusioned with the world, after years worse than wasted in chasing phantoms, why should they not turn to God? In making up an inventory at the end of the year, why should the businessman not determine to start out afresh and live henceforth on a Christian basis? " Seek ye first the kingdom of God, and his righteousness; and all these things shall be added unto you."

Since the Kingdom of God is human, it has to do with everything that concerns our lives. Largely through men and women who have enlisted for the adventure of doing God's will, his Kingdom comes to the home and the Church. That is why the two institutions exist: as training schools for the children of God, and as object lessons for other folk. What a wholesome and happy place our community would be if all of us here at home would resolve to obey the revealed will of our Lord! In such an ideal community " love is an unerring light, and joy its own security."

What, then, is the " will " to which we should look as the *summum bonum* on earth and in heaven? According to the Apostle Paul, foremost interpreter of the Christian faith, the Kingdom of God means " righteousness, and peace, and joy in the Holy Ghost." In other words, the will of the Father means the very best that he can devise for us who dwell in a world full of hatred, greed, and strife; a world often cursed by war, with all its by-products forged in hell.

During the coming year, or even during this one week, if everyone here at home would start doing the will of God, gladly and well, our part of earth would seem like the City of God. If every man or woman, boy or girl, would live as an advance agent of the Kingdom, there would be justice between man and man, peace between group and group, joy between heaven and earth. All this and vastly more we ought to mean whenever we pray: " ' Thy kingdom come.' Thy will be done in our city and to the ends of the earth! " In the words of George MacDonald, " The Kingdom of Heaven . . . is fully come when God's will becomes our will."

Thus far we have looked on the Kingdom as divine and human. It is as divine as God and as human as man.

3. *The Kingdom Is Also Practical.* It is as practical as everyday living. Sometimes our Church talk about the Kingdom sounds like " the unilluminating discussion of unreal problems in unintelligible language." Of course none of us can fathom the depths of this truth, or reach up far enough to measure its height. According to masters of Christian doctrine, the Kingdom must be both " eschatological and ethical." It has everything to do with the " final things," at the end of this present age. But at present we are concerned with the practical bearings on life in our workaday world.

" Thy will be done "! It is not only to be preached and prayed and sung. It is to be done! These four little words in our text show what it means to be a Christian: " Thy will be done "! To become a disciple of the Lord, one needs to accept him as Saviour and King. When one has taken that step, the chief business of life on earth becomes the doing of God's will. The followers of Christ as Lord may differ in heart and life as much as in appearance and ways of speech. But they should all be alike in one respect: every one should stand loyal to Christ as King. Madame Chiang Kai-shek and Dr. E. Stanley Jones ought to cherish the same sort of loyalty as the humblest

Negro washerwoman and the unknown soldier of the cross. One and all, the citizens of the Kingdom live and strive to do the will of God. " Love seems divine when duty becomes a joy."

Is it any wonder that being a Christian proves hard? In fact, apart from divine grace it is impossible day after day to do the will of God on earth as it is done in heaven. To be a follower of the Nazarene takes all a man's time, all his strength, all his lifeblood. Much of his God-given energy should go into the advancement of the Kingdom through the home and the Church. If the Lord calls a man to serve on the farm, or in the shop, that too is the appointed place for him to seek first the Kingdom of God. Such a message comes from Shakespeare in *Measure for Measure:*

> " Heaven doth with us as we with torches do,
> Not light them for themselves; for if our virtues
> Did not go forth of us, 'twere all alike
> As if we had them not. Spirits are not finely touch'd
> But to fine issues."

In our Church down South on a Sunday night just before New Year's we had as guests of honor a throng of businesswomen, together with their friends. Some of those women and girls must have been finding it hard to preserve " the white flower of a blameless life." Hence they welcomed the pastor's sermon about " The Religion of a Businesswoman." On the basis that every person's life should be a plan of God, the clergyman declared that a Christian businesswoman, such as Lydia in The Acts of the Apostles, may serve him as well as the minister at the altar or the missionary near the Congo.

The next day the pastor received a letter from a young woman whom he did not know, as she belonged to

another congregation. Here is a part of what she wrote:
" For me today and throughout the year this office shall
be the house of God and the gate of heaven. While still
a girl in college I dreamed of becoming a missionary in
Africa, like Mary Slessor. But when my father died I had
to come home and help to support the family. Often I
have almost hated this place of business. But since this
is where the Lord wishes me to serve him during most of
my waking hours, I shall strive to do my duty in the office
as gladly and well as my dear father is doing God's will
in heaven."

Such a letter raises a question that calls for a practical
answer. As we have been thinking together about the
Kingdom of God — divine, human, and practical —
more than one of you must have been whispering within
the heart: " How can I be sure about the will of God for
me personally? Evidently he has a different plan for each
of his children, and a new program for each coming day.
How can I learn the will of God for me as his child? "

The answer may lie in the text, which is part of a
prayer: " Thy kingdom come." In response to such a
petition the Father God is waiting to reveal his will for
each of his children. But remember that he always lays
down a condition. Our God is practical. He wishes any
such prayer to be sincere. If in your heart you long to
learn his will, if with all your might you stand ready to do
whatever he makes known, let your mind be at rest.
When the time comes to move forward in the path of
duty, he will open the way. Meanwhile pray, because
everything depends on him. When the hour arrives for
action, work as though it all rested with you. " If any
man will do his will, he shall know."

In the spirit of prayer and obedience you can face this

new year unafraid. You have never passed this way before, and you can never tell what another hour may bring forth. But rest assured that God knows. He cares. He is ready to make all things work together for your good, both now and evermore. Since the path of duty will soon lead you away from the doors of the church, why not bow down and commit yourself unto the Lord? " Thy kingdom come. Thy will be done in earth, as it is in heaven."

You remember the words made famous by His Majesty, King George VI, during a world-wide broadcast on a New Year's Day: " I said to a man who stood at the gate of the year: — ' Give me a light that I may tread safely into the unknown.' And he replied: — ' Go out into the darkness and put your hand into the hand of God. That shall be to you better than light, and safer than a known way.' "

PALM SUNDAY

Ps. 24; Luke 19:29–48

THE CHRIST IN OUR CITY TODAY

" When he was come near, he beheld the city, and wept over it." — Luke 19:41.

TWICE our Saviour is said to have wept. Once he shed tears of sorrow over the tomb of a friend whom he loved as a brother. Again our Lord wept tears of shame over a city that he loved more than any other place on earth. Such was the bleak background of the first Palm Sunday. Today it has to do with the coming of King Jesus into our city. If we could stand near the Dome of the Rock in old Jerusalem we might almost see Christ and his little band as they wend their way down from the Mount of Olives. Even from afar we may now behold him as he weeps over the city that should receive him as Saviour and Lord.

Let us therefore think about the welcome to Christ in our own city. At other times throughout these days before Easter, everyone should listen for the knocking of his dear hand, since the Lord Christ waits to pass through the portals of the heart where he longs to rule. Likewise should we all acclaim him as King of our nation, as well as of our world, for he alone can reign as Prince of Peace. At present we should look up to him as the Ideal Ruler of our city. From this point of view let us inquire whether or not our spirit resembles that of Jerusalem on the first Palm Sunday.

1. *The City That Welcomes Christ as King.* " When he was come into Jerusalem, all the city was moved."

These words may have suggested the opening scenes of
the Passion Play at Oberammergau. In 1930 and in 1934
some of us witnessed that mighty dramatic action, starting with Palm Sunday. Although each of the forty scenes
pointed our eyes towards the cross, both the opening and
the closing action of the drama had to do with Christ as
King. In like manner today, when we look upon him as
the Ruler of our city, let us remember that Palm Sunday
lies under the deepening shadow of the cross.

From any viewpoint the triumphal entry must have
been a sermon in action. Perhaps we should think of it
in terms of public worship. To the childlike folk who
swarmed out to meet Christ near the Garden of Geth-
semane, everything that occurred on Palm Sunday must
have seemed symbolic. The songs from the prophets
foretold the advent of Christ as King. The palms strewn
along his pathway served as tokens of his approaching
triumph. The lowly beast on which he rode proved to
the jubilant throng that he entered the Holy City as a
lover of peace. If he had been seated on a fiery charger,
gaily caparisoned, everyone would have hailed him as a
man of war.

In a Christlike spirit of humility, General Edmund
Allenby entered Jerusalem during World War I. On
November 11, 1917, after his troops had wrested the
Holy City from the Turks, the commanding officer
passed through the Joppa Gate on foot. Thus through
silent action he bade the fearful people look upon him
as a friend and a lover of peace. When once he had come
within the walls he assumed control in the name of King
George V. From that day forward, as long as the British
forces governed the City of David, they kept every street
spotless, befriended each little child, and did all in their

power to make Jerusalem worthy of its name as the City of God.

On this Palm Sunday we hail King Jesus in a different fashion. As a rule our Western religion employs few symbols, perhaps too few. But at least there can always be worship in song, which may be led by the voices of little children. Then too the reading and the preaching of the Word proclaim Christ as Ruler of our city. Sometimes there follows the confirmation of boys and girls who wish to take their stand as soldiers of the cross. For the first time in public they appear in the uniform of Christ as their King. From every point of view, therefore, Palm Sunday calls for a spirit of adoration and joy.

In view of such facts about joys unconfined, both of old and today, why should we fix our eyes upon the Man of Sorrows as he wept over the city that men called holy? Truly did he know that the hearts of little boys and girls, as well as countless childlike people, would rejoice to greet him as King. But likewise could he see hovering over that triumphal march the deepening shadow of the cross.

Today, also, he stands in our midst. Is he grateful for our songs and our sermons? Or does his heart grieve because by our deeds we crucify the Son of God afresh and put him to an open shame? " Not every one that saith unto me, Lord, Lord, shall enter into the kingdom of heaven; but he that doeth the will of my Father which is in heaven."

2. *The City That Sends Its King to the Cross.* The multitude that hailed our Lord as King on Palm Sunday must have differed from the mob that followed him to Calvary on Black Friday. Surely the little children, as

well as the women, had naught to do with nailing him
to the cross. No more had the hosts of common people
from Galilee, who filled Jerusalem and its environs at
the season of the Passover. Rather should we think of the
crucifixion as caused by a band of willful men. However
large or small the number of those who hounded the Son
of God to his death, they must have included the leading
men of that city.

Today we should pause over the question, Does our
own beloved city breathe the spirit of Palm Sunday or of
Black Friday? If the sins that crucified Jesus were com-
mitted by "respectable" men, who were guilty of envy
and wrath, is there none of that spirit among us now? If
the sins that led to the cross were greed and lying, are not
these wrongs still rife among our tradesmen? If the master evil, which embraced all the rest, was old-fashioned
politics, is that not rampant in Church and State today?
In fact, the corruption throughout our chief centers of
population once caused the foremost student of American institutions, the late Lord James Bryce, to declare
that if our civilization ever goes on the rocks the main
reason will have been the misgovernment of our cities.

Do such ways of thinking seem out of place in the
sanctuary? Not if we remember that civic scheming and
graft affect the health and morals of countless persons
for whom Christ died. Nothing human can ever seem
foreign to the heart of him who wept over Jerusalem.
Well did he know that the city called holy was like a
whited sepulcher full of dead men's bones. What must
he have thought of New York when for decades it lay
in the grasp of Democratic Tammany Hall, or of Philadelphia, which for years has been the prey of equally
unscrupulous politicians in the Republican Party?

Let us bring the matter closer home. Almost midway between those two cities lies the capital of our own state. According to disinterested observers, the politics of New Jersey have been the most malodorous in all the land. Whichever party happens to be in control seems to relish bowing down before the " boss," who serves as mayor of another city. In our state affairs for years he has wielded the power behind the throne. At present our governor keeps defying the machine, but ofttimes he appears to be helpless. His mother, one of the leading Christian gentlewomen of our time, has recently repudiated the party in which she has long served. She has also announced that she cannot affiliate with the other party because it is equally corrupt.

On this Palm Sunday, therefore, as we confess our sins, let us include those of our capital city, as it tends to crucify the Son of God afresh and put him to an open shame. From this point of view, read the words of Studdert-Kennedy about Christ in a city that the poet-preacher loved:

> " When Jesus came to Birmingham,
> They simply passed Him by,
> They never hurt a hair of Him,
> They only let Him die;
> For men had grown more tender,
> And they would not give Him pain,
> They only just passed down the street,
> And left Him in the rain."

3. *The City That Obeys Christ as King.* Even on the most corrupt and profligate of American cities, however, the doom of God has not yet fallen. Hence there must be reason for hope. When Saint John suffered as an exile

on Patmos he beheld a vision of the Holy City, New Jerusalem, coming down from God out of heaven. Early in the fifth century, A.D., when the Roman Empire seemed to be crumbling, and civilization seemed to be hovering on the verge of the abyss, Saint Augustine of Hippo composed his masterpiece, *The City of God*.

In much the same spirit of irresistible optimism a son of that Roman world has been striving to transform our largest American city. During his campaign for re-election as mayor, Fiorello H. LaGuardia publicly told the citizens, " We have a dream — to make New York heaven." Not only does he wish to take people out of the slums; he likewise proposes to take the slums out of people. The spirit of such a crusader for an ideal city resembles that of William Blake when he wrote: " To labor in knowledge is to build up Jerusalem. . . . Let every Christian, as much as in him lies, engage himself openly and publicly before all the world for the building up of Jerusalem ":

> " I will not cease from mental fight,
> Nor shall my sword sleep in my hand,
> Till we have built Jerusalem,
> In England's green and pleasant land."

What forces, then, does God wish to use in cleaning up a city that has grown corrupt and foul? Among them all he should be able to rely most surely upon the Church. In every district, and throughout the city as a whole, the influence of our congregation ought to be like that of salt, which makes for purity, and of light, which helps to transform whatever it touches. From such a practical viewpoint a municipal judge in a vile industrial city recently said to a group of local pastors: " You

church people ought to quit quarreling among your-
selves. Why don't you help your city officials to clean up
the civic cesspools? "

As a rule such influence should be indirect. " It is not
the business of the Church to create a new society," declares President John A. Mackay, of our Seminary, " but
to create the creators of that new society." Through the
worship of the sanctuary, not least on Palm Sunday, busy
men and women should catch a vision of the community
wherein old people are happy and little children are safe.
Such a city provides a winter recreation hall and a summer playground within easy walking distance of every
little boy or girl. While the older folk sit together in the
summer sunlight, according to the vision of the Hebrew
seer, the boys and girls play on the grass out in the public
park. This is only one of countless social visions that the
Lord Jesus came to transform into solid fact.

In dealing with men and women who have already
accepted Christ as Saviour and Lord, the Church ought
to show the bearing of our religion on the life of the
local community, as well as on the world across the seas.
Through preaching and teaching the Scriptures, the
Church can guide its laymen as they go out to engage
in business for the glory of God. In St. Louis a few years
ago such a man became a power in his field of manu-
facturing. At the same time he devoted himself largely
to his home and his Church. Over the desk in the private
office his pastor read a motto that showed the businessman's philosophy of life: " God first. Home second.
Shoes third."

Sometimes the Church ought to influence the city
directly. In Dallas a few years ago the firemen had voted
to go out on a strike. Before doing so, they conferred

with Pastor George W. Truett, of the First Baptist
Church. He assured them that he and his people would
do all in their power to secure for the firemen the sort
of redress that they deserved. But he implored those defenders of the city and its children not to desert their
posts of duty. Not only did they accept and follow his
fatherly counsel; from that day to this the firemen of
Dallas are said to love Pastor Truett and his home
Church.

The influence of the sanctuary ought also to extend
far beyond the limits of the city. In 1804, after Aaron
Burr had slain Alexander Hamilton in a duel, a sermon
by Eliphalet Nott in the City of Albany did much to
cause the outlawing of the duel everywhere in our land.
More than half a century later, the pulpit work of Ben-
jamin Palmer at New Orleans led to the closing of lot-
teries in Louisiana and elsewhere throughout the
United States.

In more recent years the legislature of Texas seemed
ready to pass a bill legalizing race-track gambling. Over
the week end many of the legislators journeyed from
Austin to Dallas, almost two hundred miles distant.
There on Sunday night they heard Pastor Truett preach
about life in terms of stewardship. He made no mention
of the bill in question. In fact, he did not refer to horse
racing or gambling. Nevertheless, at the church door
that night one legislator said to another, " Our race-
track bill is as dead as a salt herring," and so it proved.

In every such case the minister needs the support of
his people, as well as their prayers. Otherwise his fate
may be like that of Savonarola, who was hanged and
burned by the leaders of the city that he strove to transform. Nevertheless, such a reformer should know that

back of his cause stand both the righteousness and the power of Almighty God. " Is not my word like as a fire? saith the Lord; and like a hammer that breaketh the rock in pieces? "

In view of these facts about Christ as Lord of the city, let us remember that on the day after the triumphal entry he cleansed the Temple. In like manner now he may long to cleanse our own congregation " with the washing of water by the word," that he may " present it to himself a glorious church, not having spot, or wrinkle, or any such thing." Surely he wishes to use this congregation, like many another, as a channel through which he can cleanse and transform our city, as well as much of the world beyond. All this and more we should learn from the Gospel records about the first Palm Sunday. God forbid that the Prince of Glory should ever have cause to weep over our city!

Meanwhile the Lord Christ wishes to enter still another temple. That is your heart. In a letter to the worldliest of all the Churches in the New Testament scene, the risen Lord sends a message of hope for every erring mortal: " Behold, I stand at the door, and knock: if any man hear my voice, and open the door, I will come in to him, and will sup with him, and he with me." Before you go out to aid in the betterment of the city and the world, therefore, open up your heart and let Christ be your King. Then you can join in the song by Emily E. S. Elliott:

> " Thou camest, O Lord, with the living Word
>   That should set Thy children free;
> But with mocking scorn and with crown of thorn
>   They bore Thee to Calvary.
> O come to my heart, Lord Jesus:
>   There is room in my heart for Thee! "

MONDAY NIGHT
Isa. 52:13 to 53:12

THE GOSPEL IN TERMS OF A GARDEN
" He shall grow up before him as a tender plant,
and as a root out of a dry ground." — Isa. 53:2a.

A ROOT out of a dry ground! What does that mean?
Every gardener knows that a root does not spring up
from dry ground. Whenever you see a tender plant in
full bloom, you may be sure that the roots are in touch
with water. What, then, is the truth wrapped up in the
paradox? Simply this, that the Gospel spells mystery. A
mystery, you remember, means a divine truth that no
man is able to discover, but that everyone should gladly
accept when God makes it known.

From beginning to end the Gospel abounds in mystery
after mystery. Before any such marvel we all should
kneel in wonder and awe. One of these baffling truths
appears in our text: " He shall grow up before him as a
tender plant, and as a root out of a dry ground." These
familiar words are taken from a poem. To us as Christians, who look at the Old Testament in the light of the
New, the prophet sings about Christ and his cross. In
our text, as elsewhere throughout this golden chapter,
the seer is writing about the Saviour in terms that appeal
to the eye of the soul. Especially in the springtime of the
year, they should attract the attention of the gardener.

A root out of a dry ground! Let us translate this glowing imagery into cold American prose. The result may
be as follows: There can be no explanation of Jesus
Christ on the human level. From his birth at Bethlehem

to his death on the cross, and from his resurrection at Easter to his ascension into glory, the earthly experiences of our Redeemer abound in mystery. The mystery, however, is one of light and hope, not of darkness and gloom. If we wish to behold the mystery in something of its splendor, we ought first to consider the growth of our Saviour. The Son of the Most High " shall grow up before " the Father God " as a root out of a dry ground."

1. *The Mystery of Our Saviour's Growth.* During the period between Christmas and Holy Week, millions of us have been thinking about the earthly life of our Lord. Such meditation always proves wholesome, especially if we do not stop on the human level. But that is where we ought to start, with the tender plant emerging out of the parched earth. Though our Lord in the days of his flesh proved to be vastly more, at the beginning of his earthly career he lived on earth as the Babe of Bethlehem.

The manner of his coming to dwell among us must ever remain a mystery. " How shall this be? " said the Virgin Mary to the messenger of God before the child was conceived in the womb. Despite that fervent entreaty the angel did not attempt to dispel the mystery. He spoke about the overshadowing of the Holy Ghost, who in turn stands for the mystery of God. But why should we expect to comprehend the coming of the Most High to live among men? Since everything else about the earthly career of our Lord was unique, why should we expect to understand his birth? Should we not rather give thanks to God for the beauty of the songs that tell of his Advent? " Glory to the newborn King "!

The wonder deepens when we consider his growth into ideal manhood. Tempted in all points like other

mortals, he kept himself unspotted from the world. That
never proves easy. For example, think of the past few
months. After a winter in which the snow began to lose
its whiteness as soon as it touched the ground, we ask
how this One of earth's children, and only One, could
keep his hands clean and his heart pure. There can be no
answer, at least on the human level.

Deeper still is the mystery that hovers about the cross.
From the Christian point of view, suffering for sin rings
forth as the motif of our poetic chapter from Isaiah.
Time after time the saints of God struggle to restrain
their tears as they re-enact the scene on Calvary. Surely
it is better to bow and adore the Christ of the cross than
to sit up straight and try to explain the mystery of his
sacrifice. Over at Carr's Lane Chapel in Birmingham a
young assistant came to Robert William Dale, the senior
pastor, and complained about the difficulty of showing
the people the import of the Atonement: " Christ died
for our sins! If only I could tell them how! "

" Give up troubling, my young friend," was Dale's
reply, " about how it was possible for God to forgive sin.
Go straight and tell the people that God does forgive.
Tell them straight that Christ died for their sins. It is the
fact that people want most to know, and not your theory
or mine as to how it was possible." Dale himself was
known as a scholar and a theologian. When he gave such
counsel, he had written a strong treatise about the atonement. Because of his studies he knew that in the death
of Christ there is truth and power far above the reach of
human research. After all, what is there on earth that we
mortals comprehend?

Beyond the cross, if there were time, we might go
to Easter. Even that is not the closing scene in the drama

of redemption. Whenever we give thanks for the resurrection of our Lord we should also remember that he is coming again. What that will mean who can say? As in everything else that we know about the Redeemer of men, the Christ of the unseen future moves before us clad in robes of mystery.

All these truths, and others like them, sound forth in the noblest hymns of the Church. During the early weeks of winter we love to arise and sing: " Joy to the world! the Lord is come "! A few months later we stand up to express our joy: " Crown Him with many crowns, the Lamb upon His throne "! Which, then, of the two is the real Christ, the Babe of Bethlehem or the King of Kings? Both are real, for the two are one. Herein lies the heart of all the mystery wrapped up in the words: " He shall grow up before him as a tender plant."

Now let us turn to the other part of the text: " And as a root out of a dry ground."

2. *The Mystery of Christ's Person.* How can we hope to explain him? That we can never begin to do, at least not on the human level. In fact, the wisest of our biographers cannot account for such a man of sorrows as Abraham Lincoln or Robert E. Lee. However, it should help us to consider some of the ways in which a master of research tries to explain the achievements of such a hero.

One of those ways is that of heredity. According to Douglas S. Freeman, perhaps the ablest biographer of our time, Robert E. Lee reproduced the noblest traits of his parents and grandparents, with few of their defects. In contrast with the ancestors of that Christian gentleman, the forebears of Jesus may seem to have been

a sorry lot. Look at some of them: David, the adulterer;
Judah, the betrayer of his brother; Jacob, the sup-
planter; Noah, the victim of drink; and Adam, the
evader of his misdeeds. Once again, think of the four
women whose names appear in the genealogy of our
Lord, together with the Virgin Mother: Tamar, who
played the harlot in the family circle; Rahab, the town
prostitute of Jericho; Ruth, the immigrant from Moab;
and Bathsheba, the partner in David's adultery. Since
that sort of blood coursed through the veins of Jesus,
how could he live without sin? How could Sidney Lanier
sing about " The Crystal "?

> " O perfect life in perfect labor writ,
> O all men's Comrade, Servant, King, or Priest . . .
> Oh, what amiss may I forgive in Thee,
> Jesus, good Paragon, thou Crystal Christ? "

Again, let us think of his environment. In Athens
during the fifth century, B.C., one could have found many
a sculptor or master of public address; in Florence during the fifteenth century, A.D., many a painter or architect; in England during the sixteenth century, many a
poet or dramatist. In the time of Queen Elizabeth that
little isle is said to have resembled a " nest of singing
birds." But how different from all those places was
Nazareth in Galilee! As far as history tells, never before
or since the days of our Lord has that community sent
forth a single son or daughter worthy of note for goodness or greatness. " Can there any good thing come out
of Nazareth? " " No! " Men used to insist that the city
was God-forsaken. Such a feeling may help to account
for the fact that it became the boyhood home of Jesus.
The fact of his living there should teach us to call no
city common or unclean.

Still further, consider the growing boy's lack of schooling. Since we in the States almost worship education,
sometimes we wonder how our two noblest Presidents,
Washington and Lincoln, could rise to fame when
neither of them ever darkened the door of a university
or college. And yet either of them must have enjoyed
schooling more ample than that of Jesus. A few years
later, when the Carpenter of Nazareth dared to speak in
public, the pedants who knew him best seem to have been
astounded: " How knoweth this man letters, having
never learned? "

Much the same lack appears in what we loosely term
" culture." For example, think of travel. " The thoughts
of men are widen'd with the process of the suns." How
far, then, did our Lord ever journey from Nazareth and
Jerusalem? Except as a babe in arms carried down to
Egypt, he appears never to have traveled more than a
hundred miles from home. Neither does he seem to have
had any contacts with the poetry and the prose, the
philosophy and the art, of Athens and Rome, or of other
lands beyond Palestine. How then could he attain such
culture, and achieve such mastery of the spoken word?
That is no small portion of our mystery.

Furthermore, consider the absence of uplifting
friends. In former times, when David was young, he
found a friend in Jonathan. As long as the older man
lived young David held true to the loftiest ideals. Much
the same principle still applies to almost every man who
attains distinction. He lives up to the loving expectations
of his friends.

At Carr's Lane in Birmingham an untried young
minister once followed a succession of pulpit giants. A
visiting divine asked one of the deacons if the congrega-

tion was not running a risk. " No, sir," came the reply.
" At Carr's Lane we make our ministers." Doubtless
they employed the method that our Lord had used with
Simon Peter as a young man of promise. The way to help
such a person is to love and believe in him. Then expect
much from him in the name of his God. In short, be the
young man's friend.

But where among all the entourage of the Master do
you see a friend who could help to make him strong?
Even his mother, that good woman chosen of God, found
it hard to believe in him and his mission. What of his
other friends: Peter, James, and John; or Mary, Martha,
and the Magdalene? They found in him the secret of
the abundant life, but what did all of them together
contribute to his growth? To him those friends owed
everything good and high. In them he found almost
nothing but need.

Thus we have thought about the Man of Galilee in
terms of heredity and environment, schooling and culture, as well as friendships. Nowhere have we caught
sight of a fact that would help to account for the wonder
of his Personality. That we can never hope to do, at least
on the human level. But why should we tarry so long on
the surface of things? If a gardener sees that a tender
plant has emerged out of ground that is parched, he
knows that somewhere beneath the soil the roots have
come in touch with water. Where, then, shall we look for
the river of life that nourished the soul of our Lord in
the days of his flesh? For a suggestion looking to the
answer let us turn to a garden out in the Middle West.

In Central Kansas during August the bed of the
Arkansas River may run dry. The local sources that feed
the stream often supply no water, because there has been

no drop of rain for weeks and weeks. Nevertheless, in many an orchard or garden the apple trees are preparing to yield their luscious fruit. Across the fence the alfalfa field is full of tender plants, green and strong. If a stranger inquires, "How can these things be?" the owner of the garden and the field explains about the underflow.

Up in Colorado throughout the winter the snows keep striving to bury the loftiest mountains. A few months later the snow begins to melt and runs away toward the sea. In Central Kansas amid the driest summer, only a few feet below the surface of the ground mighty streams of living water keep coursing on their way from the mountains to the Gulf. On those unseen stores of water the farmer or gardener can depend to keep alive and thrifty any plant or tree whose roots extend far beneath the surface. In like manner, should we not look for the underflow when we try to discover the unseen sources of the grace that brings salvation through Jesus Christ? That must be what the prophet has in mind when he tells about the "root out of a dry ground." In Syria too one hears of an underground river. So let us give thanks for the underflow coming down from the hills of God!

3. *The Secret of Christ's Power.* As for his heredity, we believe that, in some way of which we know little, Jesus came from God. In the days of his flesh, again and again, he is reported to have said, "The son of man is come." Not in "trailing clouds of glory" did he come from God, who was his home, but in deepest humility. Nevertheless, he came from heaven to earth. Thus he opened the way for us back to the heart of God.

Our Lord's environment, also, was divine as well as

human. Moving about as he did, a Man among men, he was ever conscious of his Father's nearness and blessing. Never was it needful for the Man of Galilee to " practice the presence of God." To him that was more real than the things men buy and sell. What many of us experience only once in a while, it may be at " Round Top " in East Northfield, the Christ appears to have enjoyed every day, especially when he met with the Father in some quiet garden. Whenever our spirits soar until we seem to be looking over into the City of God, we may think of such an experience as resembling that of our Lord in the garden of prayer.

The same line of thought concerns his education. In God as his Father the Lord Jesus found the Ideal School-master. Is it any wonder that the Teacher of Galilee spoke as never man spoke, before or since? Among all the sons of earth, who else has been worthy to say, " The Lord God hath given me the tongue of the learned, that I should know how to speak "?

As for culture, that likewise came to Jesus through fellowship with the Living God. For many of earth's children there should be untold worth in travel amid scenes of beauty and bygone grandeur. On the other hand, such a discerning spirit as Thoreau or Whittier could find charm and even splendor near his village home. At any rate our Lord, despite his lack of " advantages," has become known as earth's most cultured Gentleman. He lived and moved and had his being in a spiritual world of his own, where God the Father was all in all.

Our Lord's friendship, too, was chiefly with the Father. Much as the Master enjoyed being with his disciples, as well as with the good friends at Bethany, be found supreme delight in communing with God. Before each important step in his career, our Lord stole away from his other friends and talked things over with his Father. Through meditation, partly in terms of the written Word, and through prayer, as the outpouring of his heart, our Saviour received strength and grace to endure all that led up to the cross. This too is what one means by the Gospel in terms of a garden.

On the human level something the same was true of John G. Paton's father. In his well-known *Autobiography,* the son and missionary to the New Hebrides wrote: " We knew whence came that happy light, as of a newborn smile, that was always dawning on my father's face. It was the reflection of the Divine Presence, in the consciousness of which he lived. Never in temple or cathedral can I hope to feel that God is more near, more vividly walking and talking with men, than under that humble cottage roof. Though everything else should be swept away out of memory, my soul would go back to those early scenes, and shut itself up in that sanctuary closet. He walked with God; why can not I? "

What, then, is the conclusion of the matter? Simply this: There can be no explanation of Christ on the human level? That was not where he lived! When we look beneath the surface, however, we find that the roots of the tender plant kept in constant touch with life-giving waters that flowed from the mountains of God. Better still, we discover that we too can keep in daily touch with those life-giving streams. Thank God for the underflow!

What an appeal such a One should make to every heart! My brother, my sister, look upon him now in all

his beauty. Do not strive to understand him, but resolve
to know him better, that you may love him more. Not
only will you find in him " fairest Lord Jesus, Ruler of
all nature." You will also learn to trust him as your
Saviour and your King.

Isa. 50:4–10; Heb. 11:32 to 12:4

THE CHRIST OF THE FLINT FACE

" The Lord God will help me; therefore shall I not be confounded: therefore have I set my face like a flint, and I know that I shall not be ashamed." — Isa. 50:7.

IF I were an artist, I should paint a picture of our Lord on his way to the cross. As a motif I should take the central thought of our text, The Christ of the Flint Face. Thus I should try to show on canvas how he excels all the sons of men in courage, in perseverance, and in power to transform the lives of his followers. In such a painting even the most casual observer should be able to behold the Gospel of the Face.

At any first-class gallery, at least in days of peace, you can study other conceptions of our Lord's personality. In Hofmann's *Christ and the Doctors,* the face has a beauty all its own. In Rembrandt's *Raising of Lazarus,* the countenance of Christ is hidden from view. In Guido Reni's *Ecce Homo,* the face of the dying Redeemer calls for tears. In many another work of art, especially from the School of Florence, you can look on the meek and gentle Shepherd, or else the tragic Man of Sorrows. But where among the galleries of Florence and Venice can you behold The Christ of the Flint Face?

A sculptor has recently made an attempt to portray the ruggedness and strength of our Lord. In 1935, Jacob Epstein displayed his statue *Behold the Man!* At once the critics arose to protest: " The Christ of Epstein shows massiveness and power beyond that of earth, but where is the sweetness and light that we should behold in the Man of Galilee? " In such a statue " there is no beauty that we should desire him." Hence it seems that we must wait for some future artist to depict on canvas or else carve in stone The Christ of the Flint Face.

At Oberammergau in 1910 and in 1922, Anton Lang took the part of the Christus, presenting him as " meek and mild." In 1930 and in 1934, Alois Lang showed the Man of Sorrows, abounding in majesty and strength. Each portrayal was in accord with the facts about the Christ. At other times we ought to think much concerning the gentleness of Jesus. At present we are to consider the more rugged aspects of his personality. From one point of view, suggested by the cleansing of the Temple, he stands forth as " The Christ of the Whip." From still another standpoint, he appears as " The Christ of the Flint Face." That is a figure of speech. What does it mean in terms of today?

1. *The Flint Face Symbolizes the Courage That Accepts the Cross.* The cross in turn stands for all things dark and hard and awful. When our Lord set his face like a flint, going up to Jerusalem, he knew from the start that every step was leading him nearer to Calvary. Where else on earth can we mortals behold courage so much like that of God?

The cross of our Lord, or of any Christian, must be voluntary. " If any man will come after me, let him deny himself, and take up his cross, and follow me." The simple words, " Take up," show that in the army of our Lord every warrior serves as a volunteer. If any soldier of our King is able to understand the will of his Leader, he knows that enlistment means setting his face toward some Jerusalem, which means the city of the cross. In the Christian life there can be no call for ninety days of an outdoor picnic, to be followed by a tour of unknown lands, with all expenses paid.

In short, the spirit of the flint face, now, as in the experience of our Lord, calls for courage sublime. Something of the perils involved appears in Dryden's " A Song for St. Cecilia's Day ":

> " The trumpet's loud clangor
> Excites us to arms
> With shrill notes of anger
> And mortal alarms.
> The double double double beat
> Of the thundering drum
> Cries, hark! the foes come;
> Charge, charge, 'tis too late to retreat."

Christian warfare, however, can seldom be spectacular. Still there is daily need of courage. " Courage is the thing! " So spoke James M. Barrie, in delivering the rectorial address at St. Andrews University. " Courage is the thing. All goes if courage goes. What says our glorious Johnson of courage? ' Unless a man has that virtue, he has no security for preserving any other.' " Courage like that of God in starting to redeem the world — such was the spirit of Christ in facing the cross. To become one of his followers means to begin doing the will of God with the heroism that Christ alone can impart, and that nothing on earth can take away.

Christian heroism proves needful in home and Church as well as on a battlefield or a Navy cruiser. In the Protestant Episcopal Church one of the wisest bishops often tells young clergymen, " Appeal to the strength of your laymen, not to their weakness." Speaking out of his own experience, the bishop calls for the courage of the cross. Once while serving as rector in a large city parish, he visited an expert with little tots of the kindergarten age and invited her to take charge of the beginners department in the Church School. She declined, with thanks: " All week I am busy with little boys and girls. On the Lord's Day I must rest. That means a complete change of thought and feeling."

In reply the rector entered into no argument, but appealed to the spirit of the cross: " Don't you think that the added work on Sunday may be your cross? " At first she did not understand. When the idea became clear, she asked for time to think and pray. Before the end of the week, she had accepted the post. Throughout the years she has proved worthy of a medal for distinguished service. The lesson that she learned must ever lie close to the heart of personal religion. To take up the cross means to choose what seems forbidding, and to start doing it now, not because one must, but because one can. Such a spirit of workaday courage must mark everyone who follows Christ.

2. *The Flint Face Also Symbolizes the Perseverance That Keeps On Bearing the Cross.* Worthy of all praise is the courage that starts up toward Jerusalem. Still more sublime is the endurance that continues true to the end. Often we have been told, " Only Omnipotence can stand in the way of a determined man." In the case before us, Omnipotence interposed no barriers along the pathway that led up to Calvary. Would that some prophet might arise now to instill in us Christians the spirit that led The Christ of the Flint Face along the way from the carpenter shop to Golgotha.

The determination shown by that Flint Face stands out in the picture by Holman Hunt, *The Shadow of*

Death. In the carpenter shop at Nazareth one beholds the Man of Galilee. Near at hand one sees the bench and the saw, the wood and the shavings. At his feet, his mother kneels beside a chest, in which she finds a crown spiked with thorns. The day has almost ended, and the " Master Workman of the race " has begun to feel weary. As he stretches out his arms to afford them rest, the light of the setting sun throws on the wall behind him a shadow of the cross.

Thus the artist shows that the whole earthly life of our Lord rested under the shadow of Calvary. From his earliest years what did our world offer him but daily calls for endurance and sacrifice? As he entered the later stages of his ministry, the shadows cast by the oncoming cross grew darker and darker. The Gospel According to St. Luke, for instance, contains six passages telling that he was aware of what awaited him in the so-called Holy City. All through those busy days of toil as Healer, Teacher, and Prophet, the spirit of the cross filled his heart to overflowing. " The Son of man came not to be ministered unto, but to minister, and to give his life a ransom for many."

Why does every follower of Christ need the spirit that shines out from the Flint Face? According to the Gospels, what does it signify to lead a Christian life? Does it not consist in a succession of days when a man lifts up the cross every morning and then bears it gladly until he lays it down at night? According to a volume of moving sermons, *The Cross in Christian Experience,* by William M. Clow, bearing the cross refers to no burden laid on a man's back against his will. The phrase points to no thorn piercing his flesh despite every effort to escape. The cross of the Christian means his portion of

the world's heartache and anguish, accepted daily and
borne willingly throughout life, according to the plan of
the Heavenly Father.

Such a spirit of perseverance and determination shines
out supremely from The Christ of the Flint Face. To be
one of his followers today means vastly more than simply
to sing about "marching as to war, with the cross of
Jesus going on before." Morning after morning, and,
much more so, late in the afternoon, bearing the cross
requires a power not one's own. How else could one endure the weight without repining, and keep moving forward gladly in the path of duty? All the while, the Christian knows that he could lay his cross down and leave it
to rot by the side of the road unless some other pilgrim
should come by and take up that weight in addition to
his own. In short, since we are observing Holy Week,
let us think much about the high cost of being a
Christian.

How can a mortal man bear his cross? Only by faith!
In the light that streams from The Christ of the Flint
Face, one sees that faith means human weakness laying
hold on divine power to supply all a man's needs. In
other words, rely on the perseverance of God! "He
which hath begun a good work in you will perform it
until the day of Jesus Christ." Such a spirit must long
have filled the heart of Martin Niemoeller's father, who
recently went home to his God. A few years ago, through
a friend in touch with Christians here in the States,
Father Niemoeller sent the following message:

"Do not let anyone pity the mother and father of
Martin Niemoeller. Only pity any follower of Christ
who does not know the joy set before those who endure
the cross, despising the shame. Yes, it is a terrible thing

to have a son in the concentration camp. Paula here [the mother] and I know that. But there would be something more terrible for us. What if God needed a faithful witness and our Martin had been unwilling?"

3. *The Flint Face Further Symbolizes the Transforming Power of the Cross.* Sometimes we sing about Christ as born among the lilies " with a glory in his bosom that transfigures you and me." But according to the New Testament, the transforming power of Christ issues mainly from his cross. For instance, listen to the Apostle Paul: " The love of Christ constraineth us; . . . he died for all, that they which live should not henceforth live unto themselves, but unto him which died for them, and rose again." In the cross, as nowhere else on earth, we can behold the glory of our God. Thus we should be changed into his likeness.

The Christ of the Flint Face has transformed the cross from a thing of shame into a means of blessing. When in anguish the Man of Sorrows moved along the Via Dolorosa, bearing his cross, the boys out in the street must have looked on him as an outcast. He was " despised and rejected of men." But now the noblest songs of praise on earth sound forth the glories of that dying Redeemer. For example, take the hymn that Matthew Arnold pronounced " the finest hymn in the English language ": ." When I survey the wondrous cross on which the Prince of Glory died."

The hour of worship in the sanctuary means most at the season of the year when we turn directly to the cross. At the Lord's Supper, above all, he makes himself known as our Redeemer and King. The Communion feast serves as our supreme memorial of saving power: " He was wounded for our transgressions, he was bruised for our iniquities: the chastisement of our peace was upon him; and with his stripes we are healed." All this can he do, and vastly more, for us and for the world, because he has made the supreme sacrifice: " This is my body, which is broken for you: this do in remembrance of me."

The Christ of the Flint Face also transforms the cross from a burden of duty imposed by others into a motive for service freely given from the heart. Instead of going forth to the day's work like a dumb beast driven with the lash, the child of God willingly takes up his cross and bears it for the sake of his Lord. Why else should Robert Moffat or Christina Forsyth have left loved ones in Scotland and dwelt in the heart of Africa, to bring to the Dark Continent the light of the Gospel? Much the same spirit of devotion to duty at any cost should mark every believer here at home. Not only did the cross stand once for all on Calvary; there is likewise a cross from day to day in the heart of every Christian.

We have now thought together concerning the Gospel of the Flint Face. That Face, marred more than any man's, serves as a deathless symbol of courage, perseverance, and transforming power. Is that not what every one of us needs today? To be lifted out of self and then changed into his likeness: such a desire fills every heart. Never will the longing prove vain if you look into the face of the Christ on the cross, and then trust in his transforming power. Herein lies the response of heaven to the plaintive words voiced by Tennyson:

> " Ah for a man to arise in me,
> That the man I am may cease to be! "

In the familiar legend of " The Great Stone Face," Nathaniel Hawthorne tells about a little boy named Edward who lived in a valley overshadowed by " The Old Man of the Mountain." Day by day the growing lad took as his ideal the strength and the poise, the beauty and the sublimity, of the face that nature's God had carved out of the solid rock. Years later, when Edward was no longer young, his neighbors and friends discovered that he had come to look like the flint face up on the mountain.

That legend is only a fantasy. But the power of the Flint Face is a fact. The Christ of the cross is able to bless, to redeem, to transform everyone who looks to him in faith. Who will turn to him now for pardon, for cleansing, and for peace? Who will trust in him for courage to start, for grace to keep on, for power to lead a new life? Who will stand up now and begin to follow The Christ of the Flint Face?

THE CROSS IN TERMS OF HEALING
" And with his stripes we are healed." — Isa. 53:5c.

HAVE you ever noticed how much the Bible says about religion and life in terms of sickness and health? It would be worth one's while to make a list of such words from the prophets and the apostles, as well as from our Lord. Especially in The Book of Psalms do these sayings abound. In the end, one would have a little book filled to overflowing with words of comfort and cheer for every person who feels sick at heart.

Why does the Bible contain much about sickness and health? Partly because these matters bulk large in the thinking of men and women who are sometimes weak and ill. Especially during the months leading up to Easter, there may be added concern about sickness and death. During the latter part of the winter, disease prevails. In February and March, death stalks our streets. Hence the obituary columns in the morning paper are often filled to overflowing.

At such a season we should rejoice that in the days of his flesh the Lord Jesus served as the Beloved Physician. Above all should we give thanks that the cross betokens his power to heal. Is it any wonder that the prophet teaches us to say, " Because of his stripes there is healing for us "? That is the way the words run in the Hebrew. If we are to understand what the seer tells about the cross, we should first think about the meaning of sin as a deadly disease of the soul.

75

1. *The Light of the Cross Reveals Sin as Mortal Sickness in the Soul.* Of course these words embody a figure of speech. In striving to make clear the awfulness of sin, the Scriptures almost exhaust the resources of language. Among all the metaphors that holy men of God have used about sin, one of the most colorful is that of disease. For much the same reason William James wrote about "the sin-sick soul." He may have learned this truth from Shakespeare's *Macbeth:*

> "Canst thou not minister to a mind diseas'd,
> Pluck from the memory a rooted sorrow,
> Raze out the written troubles of the brain,
> And with some sweet oblivious antidote
> Cleanse the stuff'd bosom of that perilous stuff
> Which weighs upon the heart?"

Any such malady affects the entire person: "The whole head is sick, and the whole heart faint. From the sole of the foot even unto the head there is no soundness in it; but wounds, and bruises, and putrifying sores." At first glance such a case appears extreme, but even where the malady seems less pronounced, every part of a man's being is likely to become affected. When poisonous bacteria begin to course through the blood stream, how can any portion of a man's body escape?

In olden times the fathers spoke about the dire consequences of sin as "total depravity." No thinking man ever supposed that any person who walked our streets was as bad as he could be. If that were the case, how could a wretch grow worse from year to year? By "total depravity" the wisest of the fathers meant that moral evils affect every portion of a man's being. When the virus of sin enters his system no part of his being can escape unscathed.

Since the virus of sin works everywhere in the blood stream of the soul, sooner or later come pain and distress. The old-fashioned name for such sufferings within the spirit was conscience. Whatever the title, every person of mature years can bear witness that when he has done wrong, and has not yet found pardon, there is likely to be in his soul unrest and agony more intense than the sufferings of his body when racked by disease. In writing of an hour when such anguish had reached its height, Milton caused one of his characters to cry out, " Which way I fly is Hell; myself am Hell."

Never do the diseases of a man's soul appear so ghastly as when he looks on them in the light of the cross. That was where Judas first became keenly aware of his disloyalty and greed; where Peter first sensed the enormity of his cowardice and lies. To the present hour, under the searchlight of the cross, every one of us can see certain evils lurking within. Far more revealing than the fluoroscope in the hands of a specialist, the cross brings to light the innermost secrets of a man's soul. This may be why one always feels humble on entering the house of God. When one looks up and beholds the cross, or else the open Bible, one should whisper a confession of sin, with a plea for mercy:

> " Be of sin the double cure;
> Cleanse me from its guilt and power."

One should also take into account a depressing fact: man's moral evil tends to infect his friends and neighbors. In fact, he may not be aware that his whole being is filled with the germs of evil, and that he is going about as a carrier of deadly disease. For instance, suppose that in days of peace one has become war-minded. In one's heart, as a citizen, the dominant impulses may be hatred of people across the border, greed to possess their soil, and bitterness because the hour has not yet come when it will seem safe to strike. In a very few years such a carrier of deadly microbes can infect a whole community, if not a countryside.

We ought to face a still more gloomy truth: unless evil is checked, it may lead to death within the soul. Here again we employ a figure of speech. In speaking about the soul, which we can never see, we must use terms relating to the body, which everyone knows full well. The death of the soul denotes being separated from the Heavenly Father; that is, from perfect Light and Life and Love. If to live forever means to be on terms of deepening fellowship with God as Father, then to die within the soul means to be severed from him. Hence Milton sings:

" The mind is its own place, and in itself
　Can make a Heaven of Hell, a Hell of Heaven."

Is there any cure for such deadly diseases of the soul? No, not by human hands! Almost every large city, such as Philadelphia or Chicago, contains a house of refuge called " The Home for Incurables." Owing to rigorous laws governing bequests, the kind men and women in charge have been unable to drop that word " Incurable." Indeed, it tells the truth, however brutally. At the present stage of medical learning, a number of diseases still afford no hope of a cure. The prognosis must be certain death. Hence the motto of such a place might be from Dante's *Inferno:* " Abandon hope, all ye who enter here."

It need never be thus with diseases of the soul. Though

WEDNESDAY NIGHT   79

more deadly by far than ills in the flesh, never does a
malady of the spirit refuse to give way before the healing
power of the cross. " Is there no balm in Gilead; is there
no physician there? why then is not the health of the
daughter of my people recovered? " Sometimes, alas, it
is because the afflicted friend never has heard of the
healing cross. Hence we turn to that brighter aspect of
the prophet's word: " With his stripes we are healed."

2. *The Light of the Cross Brings Healing for the
Deadliest Disease of the Soul.* Our word " Saviour "
might be translated " Healer." From this point of view,
which is practical, to be saved from sin means to be set
free from spiritual disease and death, thus being made
" perfectly whole." In the Early Church " when Christ
was preached as Saviour, he was proclaimed as the new
and better Healer, who could save from the sicknesses
of the soul, as from those of the body."

The cross brings power to take sin away from the
heart of any man or woman. In certain cases the treatment may be gentle, for the malady may not have become
deep-seated. But again there must be a resort to drastic
measures. If so, turn to Christ as the " Celestial Sur-
geon." Remember that Simon Peter found release from
guilt after he put himself in the hands of the One who
could heal, whereas Judas went out into night because
he turned his back on the Beloved Physician. Today,
also, " the word of God is quick, and powerful, and
sharper than any twoedged sword, piercing even to the
dividing asunder of soul and spirit, and of the joints and
marrow."

Whatever else these glowing words suggest, they declare that Christ stands ready to save unto the uttermost.

Through his death he offers life to every sin-sick mortal who turns his face toward the cross. Sometimes we sing:

> " The healing of the seamless dress
>   Is by our beds of pain;
> We touch him in life's throng and press,
>   And we are whole again."

When the soul suffers within the grasp of a malady for which there can be no cure at the hands of men, the surest way to find surcease comes through the healing cross. " As Moses lifted up the serpent in the wilderness, even so must the Son of man be lifted up: that whosoever believeth in him should not perish, but have eternal life."

If anyone asks, " How does the cross heal? " who can tell? One fact, however, we know: God loves us sinners. But he hates our sins, even more than a physician loathes the deadliest ills of the body. God has appointed the cross as the way to escape from death within the soul. Better by far than all our theories comes the witness of ten times ten thousand saints as they climb the steep ascent of heaven. Hear them singing as they onward march in the service of the King. " O God, to us may grace be given to follow in their train! "

The cross likewise brings power to renew. That must be why we love those words of the Shepherd Psalm: " He restoreth my soul." In the days of his flesh, when the Master healed the man with the withered hand, or the one who had not taken a step for almost twoscore years, immediately there came power to move and act like other folk. In like manner, through the cross, he gives the sin-free soul power to start doing the will of God, and then to keep on day after day. Who would not surrender all that he holds dear in order to be delivered from the disease that brings death to the soul? Who would not count it still more blessed to receive a new infusion of strength for Christian life and service?

When the Christ of the cross delivers a man from the evils that lurk within, he starts the new friend out on a pilgrimage for life, and then bestows on him powers equal to every task. Hence the spirit ought to be filled with joy and hope. As the days go by, the joy should increase and the hope should abound. All this may have suggested to the psychologist that arresting phrase, " The religion of healthy-mindedness." For example, behold a man who for years has been the victim of moral evils, worse by far than paralysis of the body. Then see him throughout other years as he moves about, more than a conqueror through faith in Christ. Can there be any question that he has found healing through the cross?

After such a renewal of God-given powers, the soul ought to overflow with gratitude. At Paris in 1918, one could have witnessed the first performance of *Pasteur,* a drama by Sacha Guitry. Among all the vast throng, no one listened so intently as the concierge of Pasteur Institute. That man of middle age hung on every word. During the third act, he saw that the hero was about to inoculate a little boy who had been bitten by a mad dog. Making his way backstage, the concierge breathlessly explained why he wished to see more clearly: " That's me! I was the first boy ever to be saved by Monsieur Pasteur! "

Such an act of healing, whether of body or soul, should become a personal matter. According to the Hebrew original, in the words surrounding the text the emphasis falls on the personal pronouns. Literally, then, the verse should read, " Because of his stripes there is healing for us." The healing, the cleansing, the transforming power of the cross, all flow into the heart of one person at a time. Over in a village of the Punjab, for example, there may be five thousand outcastes, or even more. If they are to enjoy the glorious liberty of God's children on earth, every one of those underprivileged folk needs to lift up his eyes and look on the Christ of the healing cross.

When shall we present-day Christians learn to speak and pray about the cross in personal pronouns? At Edinburgh University a brilliant man of science, the late Professor James Y. Simpson, loved to serve as a ruling elder in Free Saint George's Church. Ever since his death the members of the family circle have treasured his favorite copy of the Bible. In it he had underscored the passage before us now. On the margin, wherever he saw the word "our," the man of learning had put down "my." "He was wounded for my transgressions, he was bruised for my iniquities: the chastisement of my peace was upon him; and with his stripes I am healed."

My friend, have you found healing through the cross? "Yes," you reply, "years ago I came to Christ as the Physician of my soul. In the healing of his cross I found all that you have said, and vastly more. Day after day, at home and in the house of God, above all in the Sacrament, have I found peace and joy through kneeling before the cross. Never in vain have I turned to him for the balm that restores my soul and likewise makes me strong to serve my fellow men."

Thank God! That can be no small portion of what it means to become a Christian. Now there should be another question, still more searching. Have you spoken to your friends and neighbors, one by one? Have you made it clear that in Christ and his cross there is power to heal the disease known as sin? Do not make the answer to me. As we bow down for a moment of silent prayer, speak to God. Promise him that ere the setting of another sun, you will tell some friend or neighbor about the Beloved Physician and his healing cross. The hearer's response may be like that in Dora Greenwell's poem, " The Pitman to His Wife ":

" I've got a word like a sword in my heart,
    That has pierced it through and through;
When a message comes from God to a man
    He needn't ask if it's true.
There's none on earth would frame such a tale,
    For as strange as the tale may be,
Jesus my Saviour that Thou shouldst die
    For love of a man like me.

" It was for me that Jesus died,
    For me and a world of men,
Just as sinful and just as slow
    To give back His love again.
He didn't wait till I came to Him,
    But loved me at my worst;
He needn't ever have died for me,
    If I could have loved Him first."

THE SERMON IN THE SUPPER
*" As often as ye eat this bread, and drink this cup,
ye do shew the Lord's death till he come." —
I Cor. 11:26.*

" YE DO shew the Lord's death." This verb " shew " literally means to " proclaim " or " preach." In the New Testament the term appears seventeen times. In all but two cases it might be rendered " preach " or " proclaim." For this evening, therefore, let us revise the text so as to read: " As often as ye eat this bread, and drink this cup, ye do preach." Thus the subject for our meditation ought to be " The Sermon in the Supper."

The Sermon in the Supper has been repeated again and again. Even so, it should never lose its appeal to the heart. Tonight the message is being enacted in all sorts of places, from the vast cathedral to the humblest wayside chapel, not to speak of Army and Navy training camps, and lonely stations in the Mediterranean or the South Pacific. Whatever the setting, The Sermon in the Supper embodies magnetic power. The message in action brings all sorts of human beings close to the heart of God, by the old, old way of the cross, which should ever seem new and strange.

The preacher is the Church. Here tonight the messenger from the Lord of Hosts is the congregation now assembled. Through no virtue in the human agents, the sermon ought to prove the mightiest ever uttered since the Lord Christ spoke here upon earth. As long as the world contains men and women with needy souls, the

Christian Church will continue to preach The Sermon in the Supper. In the proclamation, everyone here ought to take his part, provided he loves the Lord Jesus and belongs to some branch of the Christian Church.

The sermon itself is worthy of note for simplicity. The appeal throughout comes mainly to the eye of the soul. The words appointed to be spoken or read serve chiefly to make clear what was done on the cross. That all relates to Jesus Christ. As for us human actors, " the world will little note nor long remember what we say here, but it can never forget " what he accomplished there. The sermon in the Sacrament centers about Christ. In the simplest and the most sublime of all earthly dramas, the words and the action alike point toward him and his cross. What, then, does The Sermon in the Supper teach about Christ? Three truths!

1. *The Lord's Supper Preaches the Gospel About the Christ of Yesterday.* The most important thing our Lord ever did on earth was to die. The first main purpose of the Sacrament is to remind us mortals that the Redeemer suffered for us upon the cross. To make the truth so clear and so luminous that we shall never forget, our Saviour has put it forth in the form of symbols. Hence we have a sermon in action: " This do in remembrance of me."

The bread serves as a symbol of Christ's body, broken for us. That in turn betokens sacrifice for sin. In the days of his flesh not only did our Lord give gladly of his time and strength; he likewise poured out his soul, supremely, on the cross. In some mysterious way, whenever by faith we handle the holy bread and wine, he permits us to share in his Passion.

Likewise does the cup serve as a token of his loving

sacrifice. It shows that our Lord Jesus poured out his life as an offering unto God on behalf of us sinners. "This cup is the new testament in my blood." To the Hebrews, the blood served as a symbol of life. Once again, as in taking the bread, we who belong to the redeemed family of God can share in the experience of the One who gave his all for us men and for our salvation.

The act of eating and drinking together likewise embodies a lesson. Drawn into one household of faith, we who love the Lord can show our loyalty to him by sitting at his Table. The theme of our meditation should be "The Death of Our Redeemer." The force that binds us believers together ought to be the magnetic power of the cross. Hence the Sacrament should be a "Eucharist." In it we ought to give thanks anew for him who said, "I, if I be lifted up from the earth, will draw all men unto me." Then the apostle adds, "This he said, signifying what death he should die."

In the midst of Holy Week, therefore, it is fitting that we set apart this night for the supreme sermon of the ages. Clearly and simply it preaches the most wondrous truth about the Lord of Yesterday: "Christ died for our sins according to the scriptures." Ere we enter much farther into this action sermon, we shall discover to our joy that he who once died is living now. By his Spirit he is with us this evening, tender to sympathize and mighty to save.

2. *The Lord's Supper Brings a Message About the Christ of Today.* In the midst of Holy Week, on the eve of the darkest day in the year, we ought to think of the Lord Christ as with us now at his Table. Indeed, we are here as his guests. Otherwise we might come to mourn

him around a tomb. Now we rejoice to meet him at his
Table. Too often and too much have we phrased our
religion in terms of the past. At the Table of the King,
as nowhere else on earth, we should discover that he who
once died for us lives with us here and now. He is our
Ever-present Friend, as well as our Eternal King.

The joys of the Lord's Supper ought to be like those
of King Arthur's Round Table, but on a vastly higher
level. According to old-time legends, in the sixth century
after Christ, that ruler of Britain gathered about him
the strongest and noblest knights of the land. Before he
sent them out to befriend God's suffering poor, the king
would bid them eat with him at a table that was round.
Because of that shape, no one could be exalted by sitting
near the head, nor feel abased because he was near the
foot. All the while everyone could see and hear the king.

In like manner we soldiers of King Jesus should find
joy at his " Round Table." There we can show that we
give Christ the supreme place in our hearts, that we love
all the knights who are loyal to him, and that we pledge
ourselves to his service. Just as the word " sacrament "
originally meant the soldier's pledge of allegiance to his
emperor, so at the Round Table we give ourselves one
by one to the service of our King.

We have thought about The Sermon in the Supper as
it relates to the Christ of yesterday and today. All this
we find wrapped up in the text. Also we note another
truth that present-day Christians sometimes ignore. It
relates to the Christ of tomorrow. Listen again to the
text: " As often as ye eat this bread, and drink this cup,
ye do preach the Lord's death till he come." These last
three words surely point to the Christ of the unknown
future.

3. *The Lord's Supper Brings a Prophecy Concerning the Christ of Tomorrow*. He who once died for us sinners now lives in our midst. Through the Holy Spirit, he dwells in our hearts. He has promised to come again in glory. What else do we mean whenever we repeat together the Apostles' Creed? " He ascended into heaven, and sitteth on the right hand of God the Father Almighty; from thence he shall come to judge the quick and the dead."

Once more we enter into the realm of mystery. Unless we are careful, we shall lose the trail. There is much that we cannot tell about the final return of our Lord. It is not for us on earth to know the times or the seasons that have to do with the unseen morrow. There is, likewise, much that we cannot comprehend about the manner of his coming. But of the fact itself we ought to feel sure. Beneath the shadow of the cross, this truth shines out most wondrously from The Sermon in the Supper.

The Second Advent of our Lord will mark the end of the present era, and the beginning of the golden age. Then at last the King of Kings shall have his way in the world that he died to redeem. Instead of thinking mournfully about " Truth forever on the scaffold, wrong forever on the throne," we should look forward to the time when " Christ shall have dominion over land and sea." He whose right it is shall reign for ever and ever. Hallelujah! Meanwhile we should rest secure in the knowledge that this old sin-cursed, war-blasted, sorrow-stricken world lies in the hands that once were pierced upon the cross, and that its welfare must ever be dear to the heart that once was broken on Calvary.

Thus The Sermon in the Supper stands first among all our means of grace. Through the Sacrament, our

God bestows strength, as we look back and survey the cross with its power to redeem from sin; peace, as we look about us and see once again the symbols of Christ's presence in our midst; and hope, as we think of the unknown future, when the Man of Sorrows shall be acclaimed King of earth and heaven. Whichever way we turn our eyes, therefore, we should behold the Son of God. He alone can be our Saviour, our Friend, and our King. Herein lies the mystery and the wonder of The Sermon in the Supper.

Christian friend, the Lord is about to bestow on you an honor that even an angel might covet. Christ is asking you to take part in preaching the mightiest sermon of the ages. But before you begin to do so, he bids you dedicate yourself anew to him and his cause. By faith you can help to preach the most moving sermon in history. Only by his grace can any mortal prove worthy to have a share in proclaiming this message of redeeming love. So let us look to him in adoration for his mercy.

Glory be to thee, O God, for the grace that appeared in Jesus Christ, for the power of his cross, and for The Sermon in the Supper. Glory be to thee, O Christ, for thy death upon the cross, for thy presence in our midst, and for thy coming again in triumph. Glory be to thee, O Spirit, for opening our eyes to behold the King, for cleansing our hearts to receive his coming, and for using our hands to preach The Sermon in the Supper. Glory be to thee, Father, Son, and Holy Spirit, world without end. Amen.

FRIDAY NIGHT
John 3:1–17

THE GOSPEL AS A SYMPHONY
" God so loved the world, that he gave his only begotten Son, that whosoever believeth in him should not perish, but have everlasting life." —
John 3:16.

ON THE worst of all days we turn to the best of all books. That must be the Bible. In the Holy Scriptures the most beloved part is The Gospel According to St. John. There we discover the " golden text " of the Bible. As Martin Luther used to declare, John 3:16 is " the Bible in miniature." A much more recent divine, William M. Clow, of Glasgow, shows that these twenty-four words display the dimensions of God's love, in all its breadth and its length, its depth and its height. From every point of view, therefore, our text stands out supreme, like the Matterhorn, "unmatched in all the world."

Strange to say, one rarely hears or reads a sermon about this golden text. John 3:16 seems too awesome and sublime for our human interpretations. The library of a certain minister contains more than five thousand sermons, two of which deal with our text, and only one of them reaches the heart. The difficulty seems to be that of phrasing " the old, old story " in thought-forms of our time. That is what we are now to attempt. If only by way of contrast, on this darkest of days we should think of the Gospel in terms of music. In short, the Gospel is the divine symphony of redemption.

Whenever we Christians survey the wondrous cross, our hearts ought to burst out in song. When we consider

the love of the Heavenly Father as revealed on Calvary,
some of us long for power to translate John 3:16 into
music. In certain respects these words from the Gospel resemble the *Ninth Symphony* of Beethoven. Like
that masterpiece of music, our golden text stands out
supreme. In its own fashion, also, it consists of four
movements.

In a symphony by Beethoven the First Movement
abounds with life and color, as well as onward motion.
Surely that is true of the first clause in our text.

1. *"God So Loved the World."* These five simple
words tell us mortals the most wonderful truth we ever
can know about God. We are glad to believe in him as
Light. We rejoice more in him as Life. We give ourselves
to him most of all as Love. Amid the majestic harmonies
that issue from heaven, whether on Good Friday or
Easter, the dominant note should be the love of God for
sinners. Instead of the discords that fill our war-swept
earth, we long to hear more of this other motif, the love
of God for a world in need of redemption.

Not only does the first movement of our divine symphony reveal the most wondrous truth we know about
God. The opening words of John 3:16 likewise voice the
best thing we know about the world. When we look out
over our earth, with all its tumults and its wars, we wonder how the Holy One can regard it with tenderness and
mercy. Of course we feel that he ought to be gentle and
kind with us and our beloved land. But we wonder how
he can be good to alien peoples whom we do not like.
We must confess that down in our hearts we cherish
what Charles Lamb calls "imperfect sympathies."

The whimsical essayist insists that his heart contains

" a bundle of prejudices, made up of likings and dis-
likings." He is " the veriest thrall to sympathies, apathies,
and antipathies." He acknowledges that he often finds
it hard to look with favor on certain groups of human
beings. Among them, strange to tell, he lists the Scots
and the Jews, the Negroes and the Quakers. No one else
would compile such a list as the one by Charles Lamb.
But almost every person here has his pet aversions, his
own private " index expurgatorious." Who among us
does not feel guilty of aloofness and suspicion, perhaps
even hatred and malice?

> " Alas! for the rarity
> Of Christian charity
> Under the sun! "

From this high point of view, who among us can claim
to be like God?

Especially do days of war and national rebuilding call
for Christlike love that embraces the whole earth. On
March 2, 1943, at Madison Square Garden, New York,
in the midst of World War II, Madame Chiang Kai-shek
uttered words that immediately won fame: " There must
be no bitterness in the reconstructed world. No matter
what we have undergone, and suffered, we must try to
forgive those who have injured us, and remember only
the lessons gained thereby."

Two days afterward in that same city, one of our leading psychiatrists attempted publicly to rebuke our distinguished guest: " In order to make sure of a world
properly reconstructed," said this self-appointed spokesman for our boasted " Western civilization," " we must
continue to remember with hate and bitterness the terrible evils we have suffered at the hands of Germany and

Japan." As if China had not already endured vastly more than we have ever dreamed!

From such a revolting spectacle of a Christless spirit, let us turn again to our unfinished symphony. It makes us feel that the Most High God knows naught of imperfect sympathies. The One whom we adore must be good enough and great enough to love a world cursed with sin, blasted by war, and abounding in hatred. Hence we ought to sing with Frederick W. Faber:

> " There's a wideness in God's mercy,
>   Like the wideness of the sea;
> There's a kindness in His justice,
>   Which is more than liberty."

In a Beethoven symphony the Second Movement proceeds more slowly and sedately. So is it with the symphony of redemption in the golden text of the Bible. If the first few words in John 3:16 voice the love of God for a sinful world, the second part reveals the Father's gift of his only Son.

2. " *That He Gave His . . . Son.*" When God loves, he looks in mercy both on the wicked world and the lonely sinner. When God gives, he can be content with nothing short of his best. He knows nothing of " a halfway covenant." The highest proof of his love for a world full of hatred and strife is the Gift that we know as the Christ of the cross. " God commendeth his love toward us, in that, while we were yet sinners, Christ died for us."

Words soon fail one who tries to tell what the cross meant, and must ever mean, to the heart of God the Father. The Apostle Paul, however, brings us close to the center of the mystery when he declares, " God was in Christ, reconciling the world unto himself." Like almost every other supreme text about salvation, this one traces it back to the heart of the Father God. Through the cross he longs to act as the Reconciler between heaven and earth. He alone can be the source of our redemption. In all our afflictions he is afflicted. From all our iniquities he only can redeem. That he does through Jesus Christ.

No more can mortal tongue put into words what Calvary meant, and must ever mean, to the Son of God. However, the writers of our noblest hymns do convey the spirit of the cross. For instance, take the song ascribed to Bernard of Clairvaux, " O sacred Head, now wounded." These words voice both the anguish and the glory of our Saviour's dying love. The hymn is nobly wedded to the music of the *Passion Chorale,* by Johann Sebastian Bach. In his masterpiece of heavenly harmonies, *St. Matthew Passion,* Bach employs the melody of our hymn at five different stages, each time with exquisite pathos. Where else save at the Lord's Supper can we sinful beings come so close to the spirit of the cross as in our most heavenly music?

In a standard symphony the Third Movement ought to be light and graceful. But it is not so with the next portion of John 3:16.

3. *" Whosoever Believeth . . . Should Not Perish."*
Dense as are the shadows through which we have passed, now there must be still more darkness. Here we behold a world where men and women are perishing. We must look out upon hosts of human beings who have lost their

way through life. They seem to be moving swiftly toward the bottomless pit. Hosts of our fellow men are vainly struggling to subsist without God and without hope in the world. Whatever else may be wrapped up in the word " perish," it tells of countless human beings who exist without God on earth and without hope of being with him in heaven. Even if we knew nothing of the woe that awaits impenitent sinners beyond the tomb, we ought to shudder because they are perishing all about us today.

However, let us listen more closely to the words of our text. Then we shall find unexpected reason for hope: " Whosoever believeth in him should not perish." In the light of these blessed words, why should any despair? The Son of God came from heaven to earth in quest of the lost. He died that he might lead us mortals back to the heart of his Father, both now and evermore. Through the cross he brings to the weakest and worst of human beings the offer of pardon, cleansing, and peace. Best of all, his gifts for time and eternity are free, " without money and without price." " Ho, every one that thirsteth, come " to Calvary!

No one can tell how the cross brings healing for the deadliest of human ills. Notwithstanding, from the thief on the cross down to Saul Kane, an endless procession of sinners declares that the Christ of Golgotha is able to save unto the uttermost all who come unto God through faith. As every one of us knows, in John Masefield's *The Everlasting Mercy*, Saul Kane had sunk to the lowest depths of debauchery. But when at last he stood face to face with Christ, all that was changed. Then his heart began to sing:

> " I did not think, I did not strive,
> The deep peace burnt my me alive;
> The bolted door had broken in,
> I knew that I had done with sin.
> I knew that Christ had given me birth
> To brother all the souls on earth."

Countless other object lessons of redeeming grace appear among the outcastes of India. If anyone doubts that human beings can perish here on earth, let him visit a village where hosts of " untouchables " have not yet tasted the glorious liberty of God's children here below. Then let the observer move into a neighboring hamlet where former outcastes have been plucked as brands from the burning masses of heathendom. Such an experience once brought joy to the late Bishop William F. McDowell, of the Methodist Church. While on a tour of mission stations around the world, he came to a village of India. There one night he met with forty believing men. Knowing that they all had been outcastes, he decided to test their understanding of our religion. Hence the bishop asked,

" Brothers, who is Jesus Christ? "

Instantly forty hands went up. Then the bishop singled out a man who did not look bright. At once the native Christian rose, bowed, and gave his witness:

" Sir, Jesus Christ is the Son of God, and the Saviour of the world."

" Do you all believe that? " (They nodded assent.)

" How do you know? "

Again forty hands went up. Pointing to one who looked still less promising, the bishop repeated his question. The Indian believer arose, bowed, and testified:

" Sir, I know that Jesus Christ is the Son of God and the Saviour of the world because he loved me and gave himself for me, and for all of us here, when no one else would touch the hem of our garments. If he looked on us in mercy, and then died to make us free, he must love everybody, he must be the Son of God. Only the good God would do what Christ has done for us outcastes."

When the bishop came home and told us ministers what he had heard, there shone from his eyes the glint of unshed tears. After his recital of the facts, he concluded: " It was worth going round the world more than once to hear those humble native Christians bearing witness to the grace of Jesus Christ." " Whosoever believeth in him should not perish, but have everlasting life."

In a typical symphony the Fourth Movement ought to prove climactic. It should be full of life and color. The spirit may well be that of triumph and exultation. For this reason the last movement of Beethoven's *Ninth Symphony* led Henry van Dyke to compose his uplifting " Hymn of Joy." When sung to the melody from Beethoven, that is one of our noblest hymns about the glory of God in the world about us. Especially moving are the closing lines:

> " Ever singing march we onward,
> Victors in the midst of strife;
> Joyful music lifts us sunward
> In the triumph song of life."

Higher yet should our spirits ascend as we catch the thrill of the closing words in John 3:16. They show us whither we are marching, as well as what awaits us beyond earth and time, when we have said farewell to these hills and valleys, and have crossed the river that men call death.

4. *" But Have Everlasting Life."* What, then, do we understand by " everlasting life "? Surely it means to know God as our Heavenly Father, and by his grace to be counted among his redeemed children, both on earth and in heaven. " This is life eternal, that they might know thee the only true God, and Jesus Christ, whom thou hast sent."

For the redeemed children of God, the life eternal has already begun. " He that believeth on me hath everlasting life," here and now. Everyone who has been born from above has entered into the life that will have " the glory of going on." A person who has been born anew is as immortal now on earth as he ever will be in heaven. Eternal life should be a present reality as well as a future prospect. Is it any wonder that our religion teaches us to sing, and that it leads the lover of beauty to compose majestic symphonies? As Hegel once declared, " The Divine is the center of all the supreme art."

On the other hand, the life everlasting will not appear in its fullness and glory until we enter the world beyond. There we shall be with our Lord, and we shall be like him, for we shall see him as he is, King of Saints and Son of God. " Therefore with angels and archangels and all the company of heaven we laud and magnify his glorious name, evermore praising him and saying: ' Holy, Holy, Holy, Lord God of Hosts, heaven and earth are full of the majesty of thy glory. Hosanna in the highest! ' "

Thus we have attended to the four movements in the symphony of redemption. Like all our earth-born figures, this one is by no means perfect. The analogy must be far from complete. One defect is that the person who enjoys the *Ninth Symphony* may feel somewhat passive.

Although the music should do much to transform his soul, there sounds forth no call for the listener to act.

On the other hand, when the symphony of redemption draws toward its close, it brings a summons for every listener to start moving Godward. It invites every hearer to become a " whosoever." What, then, should the whosoever do, here and now? Let him believe in Christ! That is the fitting response to his grace as revealed on the cross. Why should not every person here become one of God's whosoevers?

This word " whosoever " is unique. Like the love of God, the term whosoever embraces the world. Again like the love of the Father, whosoever refers to a single person. Over at Kidderminster in England, saintly Richard Baxter used to thank God because John 3:16 did not mention him by name. If that had been the case, the text might have referred to some other Richard Baxter, as yet unborn. Even if the author of *Saints' Everlasting Rest* had felt assured of his own eternal welfare, he could have found in this golden text no promise for anyone else. But in view of our word " whosoever," he rejoiced in a Gospel for every man or woman, boy or girl, on whom God sends the sunshine and the rain.

" Whosoever will may come." To come means to believe. Come to him now, that you may enter into life everlasting, both here and in the home above. Thus will you begin at once to share in the symphony of divine redemption.

" For God so loved the world,
that he gave his only begotten Son,
that whosoever believeth in him should not perish,
but have everlasting life."

EASTER MORNING
I Cor. 15:20–28; 35–58

THE JOYS OF THE HEAVENLY HARVEST
*" Now is Christ risen from the dead, and become
the firstfruits of them that slept." — I Cor. 15:20.*

ON EASTER morning we ought to give thanks for the
joys of the heavenly harvest. If we are to do that, we
should remember certain facts about the Holy Land.
In southern Palestine the barley harvest begins about
Easter time. Those days of ingathering prove to be the
happiest of all the year. Then if ever on earth, the children of the East rejoice with exultation like that of
heaven come down to earth.

The joys of the Hebrew farmer used to go with him
to the house of God. On the first day of the week the
harvester would bring to the Temple a sheaf of ripened
grain. That was the earliest and the best of all the ingathering. The giving to God of the first fruits served as
a token that the increase of the fields had come from
him. All the ripening grain belonged to him, and was
to be used for his glory. What a picture of a thankful
spirit on this glad Easter Day!

So much for the figure. What does it teach? When we
translate the glowing words of Saint Paul into the
prosaic speech of our time, we learn two related facts.
One has to do with our Lord; the other, with us who
believe on him. From these two facts we derive both the
music and the message of Easter Day. Amid a world that
has been at war, in a time when we often think about
what lies beyond the battlefields of earth, let us lift up

1650

our hearts and rejoice in the assurance of the heavenly harvest.

How can the children of God sing and pray when they stand beside an open tomb? Is it not because they believe in " the forgiveness of sins; the resurrection of the body; and the life everlasting "? This part of the Creed has to do with the joys of the heavenly harvest. That in turn is sure because Christ arose from the dead in the power of an endless life. The fact of his resurrection led John Oxenham to sing about " The Blessed Hope ":

> " God is! Christ loves! Christ lives!
> And by His own Returning gives
>   Sure proofs of immortality.
>   The firstfruits He; and we,
>   The harvest of His victory.
> The life beyond shall this life far transcend,
> And death is the beginning, not the end."

1. *Let Us Give Thanks to God for the Resurrection of Christ.* He is " the firstfruits of them that slept." According to the figure, his rising from the dead marks the beginning of the heavenly harvest. From this point of view the spirit of Easter ought to be still more joyful than that of Thanksgiving Day. Then we love to unite in triumphant song:

> " Come, ye thankful people, come,
>   Raise the song of harvest home."

The resurrection of Christ had to do with his body. On the cross the only portion of his personality that died was his body. When in triumph he exclaimed, " It is finished," he must have rejoiced because the sufferings of his flesh were ended. When he breathed his last, the spirit of our Lord went home to his God. Hence the dying Redeemer could assure the penitent thief: " To

Lincoln Christian College

day shalt thou be with me in paradise." Neither for the
King nor for his latest recruit was there to be any sleep-
ing of the soul. Only the body of our Lord could die
upon the cross.

Like everything else about the earthly life of our
Lord, the resurrection of his body must remain a mystery. That mystery is one of light unapproachable. In
a sense, the body of our Lord on Easter morning must
have been the same as the one that Joseph of Arimathaea
had put in the tomb on Friday evening. But from a
loftier point of view the resurrected body must meanwhile have undergone a transformation. The Person
who dwelt within was the one whose body had died upon
the cross. But after the resurrection there seems to have
been a change in his appearance, more wondrous by far
than the metamorphosis of an Easter lily. Out from a
bulb that shares the somber hues of the surrounding
soil, there bursts a bloom that makes us think of
" Paradise regained."

After the resurrection of our Lord, " the light of the
knowledge of the glory of God " kept shining out from
that blessed Face. During the forty days prior to Pentecost, he mingled at times with his followers and friends.
To them he brought a vision of the glory they would
some day behold in the Father's house. The Risen One
likewise caused their hearts to be flooded with a joy that
the world could neither give nor take away. Such ought
to be the spirit of Easter and of every Lord's Day. At the
beginning of every successive week, the First Day should
remind us that the Son of God arose from the dead and
thus brought immortality to light.

The resurrection of Christ also marked the beginning

of his reign as King. Whenever we look upon the cross, let us give thanks for him as our Saviour. On Easter, and on every Lord's Day, let us acclaim him as Ruler of heaven and earth, as well as Lord of our own hearts. Throughout the Christian year, from Easter morning until Good Friday night, let us worship and extol him as Redeemer and King, for he alone can be the Son of God. This we know because he died for our salvation, and because he lives to reign as King of Kings and Lord of Lords. Hallelujah!

Thus the resurrection of Christ marks the beginning of the heavenly harvest. One of the many differences between his resurrection and his raising of Lazarus was that Christ himself came out from the tomb to die no more, whereas the friend whom he brought from the grave had to fall asleep again. In a lofty sense the best thing we know about Jesus Christ is that he alone can be the Lord of death and the grave. Not only on Easter morning, but every day and night, the Son of God is with us. He is tender to sympathize. He is mighty to save. He is worthy to rule. Would that our whole earth might receive him today as Redeemer and King!

Joyful is the hour when the child of God discovers the living Redeemer. Then " the Jesus of History " becomes the Christ of Today. He draws near to us as the Lord of Christian experience and the closest of earthly friends. Such a discovery came to Robert William Dale early in his ministry at Carr's Lane, in Birmingham. One morning he sat in the study hard at work on his message for the approaching Easter Day. All at once there stole into his heart the assurance: " Christ is living now, and he is here." Up to that time the young clergyman had been preaching about Christ mainly in past tenses. He had tried to use the historical imagination in making vivid the drama of redemption. But he supposed that it had all occurred far away and long ago.

Then the young pastor became aware of Christ as his Contemporary. With His young friend in the study, and with the children of God everywhere, the risen Lord seemed " closer . . . than breathing . . . nearer than hands and feet." When the new light dawned on the young man's soul, he arose and paced across the study floor, exclaiming: " Christ lives! He lives! " Such was the song that began to echo in the pastor's heart. Since his own spirit had been " strangely warmed," he resolved to share the transforming vision with his friends at Carr's Lane. Every Sunday morning for weeks the message concerned the living Christ. As long as Dale ministered there he chose for each morning service a hymn about the risen Lord. Under such triumphant leadership the congregation enjoyed a sort of continuous revival. Carr's Lane became more and more of a power in the Kingdom. Thank God that every local Church can rejoice in the beginning of such a heavenly harvest!

2. *Let Us Think About the Resurrection of Believers.* That will mark the completion of the heavenly harvest: " Christ the firstfruits; afterward they that are Christ's at his coming." Once again we stand in the presence of ineffable mystery. Amid it all one truth shines forth with a glory all its own: in a world where war has been raging, and where death still abounds, the child of God can rejoice whenever he looks beyond the grave. In the life of everyone who believes in God, the best is yet to be.

How do we know? Because the Lord Jesus arose from the dead, in " the power of an endless life."

Why is Easter the most joyous day of all the year? Why should twice as many men, as well as women and children, throng the sanctuary on Easter morning as at any other time? Is it not because down in their hearts men and women keep longing for light from the land beyond the river known as death? According to an article by the lay editor of *The Christian Century,* on why men come to Church, the chief reason appears to be habit. Apart from that, says our friendly observer, they come because they wish to be sure about the life everlasting. Everywhere hearts keep longing for good news from the unseen world. Is it any wonder that on Easter morning a throng of eager worshipers fills the house of God to overflowing? It is to be hoped that they never fail to hear the Good News about the risen Lord.

What light does this glad day throw on the mystery of the beloved who are no longer with us in the flesh? According to our text, Christ is " the firstfruits of them that slept." For the child of God the experience that the world calls death must be only a sleep. What truth could be more uplifting? Think of a wee boy at the end of a happy day. Little does he regard sleep as a friend. Rather would he keep on playing with his toys. But after a while, most reluctantly, he lies down to sleep in his mother's arms. Then the weary body begins to relax. The touch of fever departs from his brow. In the early morning he will awake in newness of life. Then he will rejoice in powers equal to his tasks. In like manner are we all children of a larger growth. Hence we ought to look on death as a sleep. If death is a mystery, so is sleep, that beautiful token of the Father's love.

At Easter time the world about us seems to be full of mystery and wonder. For instance, look out on a garden. Months ago a lover of beauty placed in the soil a number of bulbs. Through the winter they appeared to sleep. But now in the springtime you can enjoy the beauty of the snowdrops and the crocus, with the fragrance of the narcissus. Later you can behold the splendor of the gladiolus. Surely " a garden is a lovesome thing, God wot! " Through this Gospel in the garden John Oxenham has taught us to see the mercy of the Lord with his children who fall asleep at the close of life's little day. The title of the poem is " Seeds ":

> " We drop a seed into the ground,
> A tiny, shapeless thing, shrivelled and dry,
> And, in the fulness of its time, is seen
> A form of peerless beauty, robed and crowned
> Beyond the pride of any earthly queen,
> Instinct with loveliness, and sweet and rare
> The perfect emblem of its Maker's care. . . .

> " For man is but the seed of what he shall be,
> When, in the fulness of his perfecting,
> He drops the husk and cleaves his upward way,
> Through earth's retardings and the clinging clay
> Into the sunshine of God's perfect day. . . .

> " Yea, we may hope!
> For we are seeds,
> Dropped into earth for heavenly blossoming. . . .

> We know not what we shall be — only this —
> That we shall be made like Him — as He is."

Beyond the sleep of the body in its earthen bed will come the awakening to newness of life. That is what we ought to mean whenever we say: " I believe in . . . the resurrection of the body." Of course we all accept the truth of immortality. Even such a sage as Socrates could assure us of continued survival after the grave. But we likewise yearn for knowledge about the future of the body. All of us feel sure that when a loved one lies down to sleep the spirit goes home to enjoy the hospitality of heaven. Should we not likewise rejoice because the body awaits the resurrection?

With what kind of body will the saints of the Lord appear in glory? Who can tell? To a limited degree the heavenly habitation may be like the one here in the flesh. The voice, for instance, need not change. If ever we become concerned about the problem of " heavenly recognition," we should recall the query of the old Scottish woman: " Do you think we'll be bigger fools in heaven than we are on earth? " There is reason even to hope that we shall recognize many of the redeemed whom we have never met on earth. If so, what a joy it will be to look on the face of the Apostle Paul! To him we are indebted for much that we know about the resurrection of the body.

On the other hand, the apostle assures us that the heavenly body will not be the same as its earthly form: " It is sown a natural body; it is raised a spiritual body." If so, thank God! What a relief! Who would wish to carry over into eternity all the handicaps and shortcomings of the flesh?

Such surmises must be of secondary concern. Amid them all, however, shines out one fact concerning which there should be no confusion: beyond the awakening in the Father's home there will be life with all its fullness and wonder. Sometimes the Book speaks of our future abode in terms of a city with wide open spaces, where fruit trees flourish beside the river. More tenderly the Master tells us about heaven as our home, into which he has gone to make ready a room for each child of the Father's love. Once again Christ bids us think of our heavenly abodes as stages in the pilgrimage from glory to glory in a world of beauty that belongs to God. Perhaps this truth suggested the couplet by Masefield:

" And may we find, when ended is the page,
    Death but a tavern on our pilgrimage."

But someone may protest: " All these sayings embody figures of speech. How can I build my hope of heaven on a metaphor, even the most sublime? " Such a question is certain to arise. While we wait for new light from above, remember that we must speak about heaven in the language of earth. Remember too that the Christian hope has more to do with the heart than the head. The Gospel is " the gift of God to the imagination." Often we can learn more about the life beyond by listening to the poet than through consulting the sage. All the while we rejoice in the assurance of life everlasting, because we believe in the risen Lord.

Sooner or later every thoughtful man asks himself why he looks forward to life beyond the grave. It seems to have been so with the late Sir Wilfred Grenfell. On Easter Day, 1908, that medical missionary in Labrador was driving his dog team across a bay. He was hastening to the relief of a man who had accidentally been shot. The doctor had supposed that the bay was frozen solid. But all at once the swiftly flying traveler found that he and his dogs were adrift on an ice floe. Silently they were slipping out to sea. Humanly speaking, there was scarcely a chance in a thousand that he would ever reach land. When he had taken a few simple precautions he began to sing the old-time hymn:

" My God and Father, while I stray
Far from my home in life's rough way,
O teach me from the heart to say,
' Thy will be done.' "

After a while he stopped his song. Then he asked himself, "Why do I believe in Jesus Christ? " The doctor concluded that his chief reason lay in the resurrection. Some such practical conception must have been in the mind of the Apostle Paul when he wrote at the end of his triumphant Easter Chapter: " My beloved brethren, be ye stedfast, unmoveable, always abounding in the work of the Lord, forasmuch as ye know that your labour is not in vain in the Lord."

Once in a while a strong man asks himself: " Is life good? Is it worth all it costs? " For the Christian there can be only one reply: a glorious " Yes! " To live as a member of God's redeemed family here below means that like Saint Paul and Wilfred Grenfell you are helping to raise the seed corn for the coming of God's Kingdom on earth. Therefore you can rest assured that your labors for Christ can never be in vain. " Whatsoever a man soweth, that shall he also reap."

The Lord of the eternal harvest wishes everyone here to have a bountiful share in these joys of earth and heaven. The chief assurance of God's blessing for time and eternity is the resurrection of our Lord. " Now is Christ risen from the dead, and become the firstfruits of them that slept." " Every man in his own order: Christ the firstfruits; afterward they that are Christ's at his coming." Thank God for your own portion of the joys in the heavenly harvest!

EASTER VESPERS
Luke 24:13–35

THE SECRET OF CHRISTIAN RADIANCE
*" Did not our heart burn within us, while he
talked with us by the way, and while he opened
to us the scriptures? " — Luke 24:32.*

THIS evening we rejoice in the afterglow of Easter
morn. Rightly do we regard this day as the most wondrous in all the year. Now that the night draws nigh we
are wondering how we can receive such inspiration and
uplift at the beginning of every week. Should we not set
apart every Lord's Day as a memorial of the resurrection,
and thus enjoy foretastes of the life everlasting? Indeed,
why not let all our days on earth be bright with the glory
of Easter morning? That is the ideal. What are the facts?

Many of us appear to be like those two pilgrims on the
dusty road to Emmaus. We have lost the wonder and the
thrill of our religion. We try to endure what we should
enjoy. Even on this glad day we often speak about
" the lost radiance of the Christian religion." In 1924 a
book under that title came from Dr. L. P. Jacks, of London, a brilliant editor and a lover of the Church. During
the past twenty years the tone color of our religion has
not changed, at least not for the better. We still pitch
many of our hymns in a minor key. We continue to
phrase much of our preaching in gloomy past tenses.
Hence a good deal of our religion appears to be second-
hand, if not shopworn.

With John Bunyan some of us might confess: " We are
a company of worn-out Christians. Our moon is on the
wane. We are much more black than white, more dark

than light. We shine but little. Grace in most of us is decayed." If so, do we forget that our religion ought to be luminous with the sunlight of the Resurrection? How, then, can we hope to recapture our lost radiance? The experience of the two disciples on that dusty road shows how we can find the treasure we have lost. Such an experience may consist of four elements, each of which will bring us close to the risen Lord.

1. *Christian Radiance Comes Through Fellowship with the Living Christ.* Those two hearts began to burn as soon as the pilgrims fell in step with the Lord on Easter Day. So ought it to be whenever husband and wife come with Him to the sanctuary for prayer and praise. As Oliver Wendell Holmes used to insist, every normal heart contains a growing plant called reverence, which needs to be watered at least once a week. When we engage in the worship of God's house, the spirit of the hymns and the prayers, as well as the readings from the Book and the message from the pastor, ought to lift us out of ourselves and lead us to the mountaintop. There we should behold the face of our King and be transformed into his likeness.

Fortunately, we can enjoy such fellowship almost anywhere throughout the week. The friends in view were walking along a dusty highway. So can every Christian " practice the presence of God " out on the open road. Why should not every believer today form the old-fashioned habit of singing about Jesus while hard at work? Especially at Easter time, when our world has been reeling because of war, some of the songs on the dusty road should concern the risen Lord and the life to come. Since our religion calls for a deepening friendship with

the Christ of today, how can we know him well and love
him much unless we walk with him along life's busy
road?

Over in the heart of Africa, David Livingstone found
the secret of Christian radiance. Day after day he strug-
gled on through swamp and forest. Beset by perils on
every side, oppressed by burdens of many sorts, far from
the sound of a white man's voice, Livingstone entered
daily into " the peace of God, which passeth all understanding." By experience he learned that serenity and
joy never failed to come when he sang to himself the
noblest of the psalms and hymns. Especially did he love
to sing and to say the Latin form of the words ascribed
to Bernard of Clairvaux:

> " Jesus, the very thought of Thee
> With sweetness fills my breast;
> But sweeter far Thy face to see,
> And in Thy presence rest."

2. *Christian Radiance Comes Through Understanding the Bible.* " Did not our heart burn within us . . .
while he opened to us the scriptures? " From earliest
childhood those two pilgrims must have known much
about the Book. Glibly could they recount what others
had taught them about God in Christ. Nevertheless, on
that Easter afternoon the risen Lord opened the Bible
so that its glory shone into their faces as never before. He
also opened their eyes to behold the " vision splendid,"
and their hearts to receive the shining truth. Thus he led
them into " a brave new world." Henceforth their hearts
would burn and their lives would glow. In much the
same fashion, the Christ of today longs to open up the
Scriptures for all of us. Then there will be a new fire in
many a heart, and a new radiance in many a life.

Such a discovery came to Dr. L. P. Jacks when past fifty years of age. In his recent book, *The Confessions of an Octogenarian*, he acknowledges that he had served as a minister of the Gospel a quarter of a century before he learned to look on the New Testament as a whole. During those twenty-five years he had learned much of what the scholars had written about the Bible. With other men of repute he had thought of the New Testament as "a collection of books rather loosely put together, all having to do with Jesus Christ, but in ways not in harmony with each other." When at last the eyes of that earnest reader were opened, he began really to study the Bible for himself. What did he discover as the unifying truth of the New Testament? The fact of the Living Christ!

On the road to Emmaus the two pilgrims learned to see Christ in the Old Testament. If so, we surely ought to find him in the New. Even there, do we look upon him as the Lord of today? According to Dr. Jacks, the religion of the New Testament centers round the truth of eternal life for "the believer in Christ as risen from the dead." Such testimony comes from a brilliant thinker who styles himself a Unitarian. Instead of accepting his findings, however, why not search the Scriptures to see whether or not his report about the facts is correct? If you let the Spirit of the risen Lord guide in reading the Book, you will find much that will cause your heart to burn and your face to shine.

3. *Christian Radiance Comes Through Enlisting for Service*. As John Ruskin used to say, the Bible is a Book no syllable of which can be understood apart from a deed. Christian radiance appears to be only

another title for "the illumination of obedience." If those two disciples had attempted to keep their discovery a secret, the fire would have died down in their hearts, and the glow would have faded from their faces, before that first Easter Day had deepened into night. Is it any wonder that the Apostle Paul closes his Resurrection Chapter with an appeal for us Christians to be "always abounding in the work of the Lord"? Then he goes on to speak about "the collection for the saints." What a practical Christian idealist!

If you would know the joys of the Resurrection Gospel, enlist at once in the service of the risen Lord. Among all your friends and acquaintances, who are the happy folk? Are they not men and women who, like their Master, go about doing good? Not all earth's toiling millions, alas, have learned how to labor with joy. More than a few are being crushed beneath burdens too heavy for mortals to bear. Nevertheless, Henry van Dyke came close to the heart of the truth when he wrote, "The blessing of earth is toil." For anyone who has learned the inner meaning of the Christian faith, life in God's world can never become a treadmill. Still less will earthly existence seem like a merry-go-round. Rather does the spirit of Easter Day summon the believer to heroic service for Christ and fellow men.

Why not call the roll of the most radiant believers you have ever known and loved? Near the top of the list be sure to put the names of certain missionaries. Because of the heat, the squalor, and the loneliness of some foreign outpost, many an advance agent of the Kingdom has learned to enjoy fellowship with the Living Christ, to walk with him as he opens the Scriptures, and to share with others the fire that he kindles in the heart. The radiance of such a young missionary wife and mother caused a woman traveler from the States to write an unusual letter:

" I never have met you personally, but I know your daughter here in China. She is one of God's flowers, blossoming here where she is sorely needed. I hope that my letter will start in your soul a hymn of gratitude. Your daughter I found, not on God's altar, but living as a child of the King, and being wonderfully used by him. There is in the heart of the missionary a joy that few of us back at home have found. Now I understand something about the multiplying of the loaves and fishes. I have witnessed a marvelous multiplying of the pitifully small provision we have put in the hands of His servants over here in China." Something of the same serenity and joy breathes out from the poem by John Masefield called " The Seekers ":

" We seek the City of God, and the haunt where beauty
     dwells,
And we find the noisy mart and the sound of burial bells.
· · · · · · · · · · · · · · · · · ·

" We travel from dawn to dusk, till the day is past and by,
Seeking the Holy City beyond the rim of the sky.

" Friends and loves we have none, nor wealth nor blest
     abode,
But the hope of the City of God at the other end of the
     road."

4. *Christian Radiance Comes Through Abiding in Hope.* On Easter morning why were those two disciples sad and disconsolate? Because they were trying to live without hope. In former times they had begun to look upon Jesus as their Deliverer. When they learned that he was dead, they could see no ray of light. They must

have asked, " How can a dead Christ redeem? " Instead of going forward with joy in his service, they had begun to look backward, and to feel sorry for themselves. From that day until now, whenever believing men and women have lost their assurance of the living Lord, they have given up hope. When God's children bid farewell to hope, they succumb to all sorts of soul diseases, especially despondency.

We are thinking about professing Christians, whom the world rightly terms " good." Like those two friends on the dusty road, many who yield to gloom do not feel weighed down by any sense of unforgiven sin. Despite the fact that they believe in God's redeeming grace, they act as though life were only an endless succession of heartaches and apprehensions. They have formed the habit of looking back, of looking down, of looking within. Hence earth's pilgrimage seems likely to stop any day in a dead-end street. Sometimes they ask each other, " Is life worth all it costs? " To any such query the reply may come sharp and clear: " No! Life without hope must lead erelong to bankruptcy of the soul."

On the other hand, the spirit of Easter should be radiant with Christian hope. This day bids us sing and preach the Gospel of the upward look. The Resurrection teaches us to center religion and service in the Christ of today and tomorrow. Does such a way of regarding life seem otherworldly? If so, remember that the early Christians believed in heaven. At the same time they were intensely practical. Those radiant believers translated " apostolic optimism " into achievements so mighty that they put us to shame. Their heathen neighbors said that those Christians had turned the Roman world upside down. Would that their example might lead to the recovery of our lost radiance! Then our hope in the Christ of tomorrow would bring us power to serve the Christ of today. With new strength and hope would come new joy and peace.

Why did the afterglow of the first Easter flood the Apostolic Church with light from above? Listen to Friedrich Heiler, who has made a special study of Christian worship: " Never again in the history of the Church, or of religion in general, has the life of worship revealed such power, such depth, and such fruitfulness as in the earliest times." That new influx of power, that rare effulgence of glory from God, came to the Church because the saints lived in the light of the Resurrection. As long as those believers rejoiced to serve in that light, with its hope of the Kingdom to come, their hearts and their lives overflowed with power and joy.

What does the Christian hope include? Everything good and high, on earth and in heaven! In the afterglow of Easter Day the child of God looks forward to the triumph of his Kingdom among men and nations, to the increasing glory of the Church as God's agent in redeeming the world, and to the life everlasting for every true believer in the risen Lord. At a time when war has been raging, and has left a vacant chair in many a family circle, with a lonely grave on many a distant battlefield, have we who tarry in the flesh no need of the Living Lord? The Christ of today and tomorrow alone can declare: " I am the resurrection, and the life: he that believeth in me, though he were dead, yet shall he live: and whosoever liveth and believeth in me shall never die."

This evening, as day is dying in the west, one tends to think of life as drawing to its close. For light on such mysteries one may turn to John Buchan, the late Lord

Tweedsmuir. In one of his moving tales of adventure he quotes a plain man from Kentucky, to whom death is drawing near: " I reckon it's like going to sleep when you are tired out, and waking to find a summer morning with the scent of the hay coming in at the window. I used to thank God for such mornings back in the blue-grass country, and I shall thank Him when I wake up on the other side of the mountain."

Looking back now, we can recall four main factors that enter into the experience of Christian radiance: Fellowship with the Living Christ, Understanding the Bible, Enlisting for Service, and Abiding in Hope. Such an experience came to the pilgrims on the dusty road to Emmaus. Why, then, should we sigh after " the lost radiance of the Christian religion "? Should we not rather determine, one by one, to live and serve in the afterglow of Easter? Such is the vision of Christina G. Rossetti:

> " My life is but a working day
>   Whose tasks are set aright.
> A while to work, a while to pray,
>   And then a quiet night.
> And then, please God, a quiet night
>   Where saints and angels walk in white,
> One dreamless sleep from work and sorrow,
>   But reawaking on the morrow."

PENTECOST DAY

Ezek. 37:1–10; Acts 1:1–8

THE SPIRIT AMONG DRY BONES

*" The hand of the Lord was upon me, and carried
me out in the spirit of the Lord, and set me down
in the midst of the valley which was full of bones."
— Ezek. 37:1.*

PROPHECY comes as the gift of God to the imagination. The old-time Hebrews were a childlike people.
They learned easily what they saw clearly. When Ezekiel
told them about the valley full of bones, the Children
of Israel had gone into exile. Through this vision they
discovered that they could still hope in God. In Old
Testament history the vision related to the return from
the Exile. For us as Christians there may also be a wider
meaning. At any rate there is a striking resemblance between the valley full of dead men's bones and many a
portion of our earth today.

Over in that Eastern world behold a valley long and
wide. Years ago two vast armies had come together in
mortal combat. After days of indecisive battle, both sides
retired, leaving the dead to bury the dead. In the course
of time the vast valley seemed to be full of dead men's
bones, very many and very dry. Without pushing the
analogy too far we may think of that scene as resembling
vast stretches of earth today. If so, the dry bones may
symbolize dead souls. Could any spot be more desolate?
Could any portion of earth seem more God-forsaken?
Nevertheless, into that valley of bones came the quicken-
ing power of the Holy Spirit.

Such a message accords with the Day of Pentecost. At
this season of the year we ought to think much about the

Spirit of God, especially in terms of power. Of course he must be far more. He is also divine wisdom and perfect beauty. But when one stands in the midst of a valley full of bones one needs something more than wisdom and beauty. One must have power, the power of God. Let this therefore serve as the central thought of the present discourse: The Holy Spirit means the power of God in the lives of men, for service.

1. *The Power of the Holy Spirit.* The prophets never seem more impressive than when they write about religion in terms of power. Ezekiel, for instance, tells how God can change the stony heart and make it tender, like that of a child. Again the seer draws a picture of religion as an irresistible river, which broadens and deepens in its onward sweep until at last it brings life to the Dead Sea. In the passage before us the man of God writes of the Spirit's power in terms of the wind. When we deal with any such figure of speech, first we translate it into fact, then we interpret the fact in the light of the figure.

Throughout the Old Testament the word rendered " spirit " literally means " wind." In the New Testament the same holds true, though of course the term in the Greek differs from the corresponding word in the Hebrew. Whenever the Bible speaks about the wind, figuratively, we should think of the Holy Spirit. In talking with Nicodemus, for example, Jesus said: " The wind bloweth where it listeth." As if in answer to the unspoken question about what he meant, the Teacher explained his words: " So is every one that is born of the Spirit." Other symbols of the Holy Spirit's power include fire and light. Whatever the form of the teaching, the heart of the truth about the Holy Spirit has to do with power.

The power of the Holy Spirit must be practical. He can open the eyes of a man to behold what lies hidden from other mortals. The Holy Spirit can use a man's preaching to quicken dead souls into life. If such words seem to be full of mystery, so is the Holy Spirit. Who among us understands the ways of the wild west wind? " Thou hearest the sound thereof, but canst not tell whence it cometh or whither it goeth." Who can account for the transforming power of water in the desert, or of fire among metals? Who knows how light works as if by magic? Still less can any mortal hope to comprehend the mystery of the Spirit's power.

One fact, however, shines out clearly: The power of the Holy Spirit is wielded by a Person. The name of that Person is God. In the passage before us, and elsewhere in the Scriptures, the Holy Spirit utters words that come only from God. The Spirit performs works that call for the infinite resources of the Almighty. The Spirit receives the sort of homage that we reserve for the Most High. In short, amid all the mysteries of our religion, few can equal this one concerning the Holy Spirit as the Power of God.

2. *The Power of the Holy Spirit Through Preaching.* According to the vision, our prophet heard the Spirit's call: " Prophesy upon these bones." In words of today, " Preach to dead souls." In much the same fashion one of the fathers spoke of the time for the sermon as half an hour in which to raise the dead. More recently Dr. James Black, of Edinburgh, has written an unusually helpful book about *The Mystery of Preaching*. From our side of the water a still later volume deals with *The Miracle of Preaching*. The mystery has to do with the preacher's

source of spiritual power. The miracle concerns the life that preaching brings into the valley full of dead men's bones.

What, then, has the Holy Spirit to do with preaching? Everything good and high! He alone has the right to determine where a man shall preach. According to the vision, the Spirit set the prophet down in the midst of a valley that seemed to be God-forsaken. The same power of God led Simon Peter to address the throng at Pentecost, and Deacon Philip to do personal work with the eunuch on his way homeward to Ethiopia. In modern times the Spirit led John L. Nevius to labor in China, and S. Hall Young to work in Alaska. Each of those men had expected to serve God in the field to which the Spirit guided the other. Thus the power of God " moves in a mysterious way, his wonders to perform." He may even send a frail seer to preach in a lonely valley full of dead men's bones.

The Spirit likewise determines what the servant of God shall do for dead souls. Shall he devote himself to an exhaustive study of the battlefield where two vast armies have engaged in mortal combat and have left the field strewn with their unburied dead? Shall he send out for additional laborers to help him to give the dry bones a respectable burial? Much to our amazement, the Spirit of God appears to be little concerned about many things that we count practical. Rather does he sound a call that would seem absurd if it did not come from God: " Prophesy upon these bones! " When you are set down in a place that seems God-forsaken, stand up and preach the Gospel to dead souls!

" What shall I preach? " Listen! The Spirit of God is speaking: " Say unto them, ' Ye shall live; and ye shall

know that I am the Lord! ' " The mystery of preaching
has to do with life from the dead. The miracle of preaching concerns the change of dead men's bones into living
souls. Whatever these metaphors mean in detail, they
tell us that preaching calls for the use of powers higher
than anything known on earth. Instead of treating a sermon as merely " animated conversation " about things
of mutual concern between pulpit and pew, the Spirit of
God leads the appointed spokesman to bring into Death
Valley a message of life and hope.

Still further, the Holy Spirit alone has the right to
determine how a man shall preach. Here too we stand in
the presence of mystery. Every spokesman for God should
be himself. Both in substance and in form his message
ought to be his own. Hence it should differ from that of
every other herald. Nevertheless, the servant of the Most
High should not look on himself as a free agent. When
the Spirit bids him bring the dry bones a message of life
from the dead, woe be to him if he substitutes anything
made by man. Rather should the preacher humble himself and serve as the messenger of God. " Thus saith
the Lord! "

Throughout the history of preaching the stress has
often fallen upon power. In Old Testament days the
mightiest of all the Hebrews were the prophets, every
one of whom was a preacher. In New Testament times,
at least after Pentecost, the chief spokesmen for Christ
were even more dynamic than the prophets. According
to the Apostle Paul, it pleased God to save men through
" the foolishness of preaching." From that day to this,
whenever the tides of religion have risen toward their
flood, the Church has made a rediscovery of preaching.
According to Professor H. H. Farmer, of Cambridge,

England, one of the most hopeful signs on the world horizon today is the rediscovery of preaching as the power of God.

Ofttimes the Spirit of God works through a humble messenger whose name never appears in the headlines. Perhaps he toils for years in a foreign mission station that seems as hopeless as a valley full of bones. Such was the case with a nameless missionary in one of the Fuegian Islands. When Charles Darwin visited that part of the South Pacific, the young scientist from England declared that the natives seemed almost inhuman. He did not believe that any power on earth could ever change them into assets instead of liabilities. Within less than a generation the scientific observer acknowledged that he had been mistaken. As a token of his admiration for the wonders wrought by a nameless Christian worker, the nonbelieving scientist sent the London Missionary Society his personal check for five pounds. Such an action speaks louder than words. Try it!

3. *The Power of the Spirit in Response to Prayer.* Preaching calls for the use of power. But preaching alone can never be enough. According to our vision, after the man of God had prophesied over the dry bones, there followed a vast commotion. Soon the valley was filled with dead men's bodies. They were perfectly whole, but still they were dead. Without pressing the figure unduly, we infer that preaching should cause reform. In China and India, as well as other parts of the non-Christian world, the proclaiming of the Gospel has led to tremendous social upheavals. India and China will never again be the same. All that is good as far as it goes. But preach-

ing alone cannot bring life to dead souls. That calls for still more power. It too must come from above.

Hence the vision leads up to another stage, which is climactic. " Prophesy unto the wind! " In other words, " Pray for the Spirit! " Here again we stand in the presence of the vast unknown. However, we can see that the bringing of life from the dead must rest with the Holy Spirit. He has chosen to impart this power to us in response to prayer. So it seems that in the miracle of the Gospel the Spirit of God must be all in all. From beginning to end the laborer in the valley of bones ought to follow his bidding and lay hold on his power. In the vision before us, when the servant of God had preached and prayed, as he was commanded, those dead bodies sprang into life. " They stood up upon their feet, an exceeding great army." That is what we long to witness on every mission field. Of late such tidings have been coming from Brazil.

In performing miracles of grace the Lord God never repeats his ways of working. There can be no way of foretelling how the Holy Spirit will communicate his power. Nevertheless, in every revival worthy of the name, the power has come mainly through the two old-fashioned channels, prayer and preaching. Was it not so at Pentecost? There the supplications for power from on high and the preaching of the truth from God led to a transformation even more wondrous than that in the valley of dry bones. Hence we ought to think of Pentecost as the day of the Holy Spirit.

" But Pentecost took place in the Holy City! What has all that to do with the valley full of dead men's bones? " For one of many answers turn to John Bunyan's treatise

The Jerusalem Sinner Saved. There the seer of Bedford shows that the so-called " Holy City " had served as " the slaughter shop for saints." The hundreds of thousands of Hebrews who assembled for Pentecost included some of the worst sinners then on earth. As Bunyan reminds us, the first sermon after the ascension of our Lord was addressed to " the vilest of men," even the murderers of Jesus Christ. Where could one find a more " God-forsaken " situation? Nevertheless, at Jerusalem those men preached, in the spirit of prayer. Then the power of God employed both preaching and prayer as the means of saving those " Jerusalem sinners." Behold what God hath wrought!

Thus we have considered the Holy Spirit in terms of power. The power of God comes to dead souls through preaching and through prayer, both by his appointed servant. Since the Church today stands sorely in need of power, why do we not look to the Source? At the East Northfield Bible Conference some years ago a well-known clergyman was lecturing every morning before the main assembly. To his amazement, one evening he was asked to speak the next day before a group of three hundred ministers. Since he was at a loss about what to say, he consulted a godly woman whose father had been closely associated with Dwight L. Moody. To her the visiting divine explained his dilemma. It sprang from his inability to pack into a single hour all that he wished to tell his brother ministers. When she learned the cause of his perplexity, her eyes began to fill with tears. Then she replied:

" Tell them about the Holy Spirit! In the olden days here with Mr. Moody we used to sing and pray about the Spirit of God. The men on the platform gave him a large

place in their sermons. In these latter days we seem to
have lost much of that old-time power and joy. Do ask
the ministers to preach and to pray in the power and joy
of the Holy Spirit! " Is there no need for such words of
wisdom today?

My friend, do you ever feel helpless in the face of a
world that has been cursed with war? Do you ever ask
yourself: " Can there be any hope for the people among
whom I labor? How can they have power and joy when
God seems not to be in all their thoughts? " If such a
dark mood ever begins to steal over your spirit, turn to
this vision about the valley full of dead men's bones.
Remember that the bones represent dead souls.

Amid your own valley of vision listen for the voice of
the Holy Spirit. In a world where sin and death abound
he is able to bring life and hope. Of ourselves we in the
Church can do nothing for dead souls. But when we trust
in the power of the Most High God we discover that the
Holy Spirit can transform the valley full of bones into a
field that is filled with an exceeding great army of the
redeemed.

The Holy Spirit still means the power of God in the
lives of men, for service. To you he is saying now, as to
the prophet of old: " Stand upon thy feet, and I will
speak unto thee."

TRINITY SUNDAY

John 14:1–18, 27

THE TRINITY IN OUR EXPERIENCE

" The grace of the Lord Jesus Christ, and the love of God, and the communion of the Holy Ghost, be with you all." — II Cor. 13:14.

" THIS benediction of the Christian Church never grows old and never becomes monotonous. It is like the sunshine, which rises on us every day of our lives with a fresh beauty, or like our truest friendships, which are forever new." So spoke Phillips Brooks, for twenty-two years the beloved rector of Trinity Church in Boston. On every Lord's Day he strove to undergird his preaching with the doctrine of the Triune God. Especially on Trinity Sunday did he take delight in preaching the truth from which his Church derived its name. That doctrine seemed to him both "the center and circumference of our faith."

Our clearest statement about the Trinity appears in the Apostolic Benediction. Let us remember that our text is a benediction, not simply a prayer. Again and again at the close of public worship the minister invokes the favor of the Triune God. In pronouncing the benediction the man ordained by the Church blesses the assembled people. He addresses the holy words to men and women, not to God. Therefore he extends his hands upward, with palms reaching down, as if to cover with the divine mercy those who bow to receive the Lord's blessing. In a prayer, if the minister uses his hands at all, he lifts the palms up toward heaven. Thus we have in symbolic action the angels of God ascending and descending. When they bring the mercies wrapped up in the benediction, the hour of worship is complete.

At the heart of the benediction lies the truth of the Trinity. As we learn from the Apostles' Creed, this teaching undergirds the Christian faith: " I believe in God the Father, . . . and in Jesus Christ His only Son. . . . I believe in the Holy Ghost." In fact, this truth about the Trinity undergirds all the Scriptures. The Old Testament reveals the glory of Him whom we know as God the Father. The Gospels make known the Father through the Son. The latter portion of the New Testament reveals the Father and the Son through the Holy Spirit. Thus we are making the facts appear unduly simple. But still we can never go astray in reading the Scriptures if we look aright for God the Father, the Son, and the Holy Spirit.

1. *The Trinity in Christian Thinking.* What, then, do we Christians understand by the Trinity? According to a wise theologian, James Denney, of Glasgow, this truth serves as " the fundamental doctrine of our faith." As a loving pastor, Phillips Brooks speaks more simply. He refers to the Trinity as " a description of what we know about God." Brooks likewise warns us not to presume: " We have no right to say what God is in Himself, for there is much in Him that we cannot know, at least not yet." Meanwhile, he insists, we ought to look on the Trinity, " not as a puzzle or a satisfaction of the intellect, but as an expression of the manifold helpfulness with which the divine nature offers itself to human need."

Such a way of approaching the doctrine has more to do with the heart than the head. Throughout nineteen hundred years men have striven to make the teaching clear.

They have devised all sorts of analogies, including these: the body, the mind, and the soul of a man; the heat, the light, and the radiance of the sun; the root, the branches, and the trunk of a tree. Such comparisons fall far short of the truth wrapped up in our word Trinity. How can we mortals hope to picture the mystery of God by using things on earth?

Nevertheless, analogies sometimes prove helpful. If so, they appeal to the imagination, which sees so clearly that one cannot forget. In Ohio, for instance, an esteemed elder recently told of a message that he had heard as a growing lad, fifty years before. On a Lord's Day when the ground was covered with snow, the parish minister preached about the Trinity in terms of snow, ice, and water. Through all these years, whenever that layman has beheld the Gospel in the snow, he has given thanks for the simple message about the " Blest One in Three."

The minister would have taken his stand on firmer ground if he had derived his ideas from a first-class hymnal. There he would have found a number of songs about " The Trinity." The first of these hymns may be the one by Bishop Reginald Heber, " Holy, Holy, Holy." The heart of it all sounds forth in the closing words: " God in Three Persons, blessed Trinity."

Another song of praise moves on a lower level as poetry, or as music, but in it all the truth concerning the Trinity rings out still more distinctly. In the well-known hymn, " Come, Thou Almighty King," the first stanza appeals to God the " Father All-Glorious "; the second, to Christ, the " Incarnate Word "; the third, to the Holy Spirit as the " Comforter "; and the fourth, to " the great One in Three." Here again the stress falls on the Trinity in our experience.

The same truth appears in the rite of Christian baptism. Such a sacred ceremony constitutes a sermon in action. If so, the text may be that one about " the name of the Father, and of the Son, and of the Holy Ghost." By grace the minister invokes on the candidate the blessing of the Triune God. By faith the man who comes into the Church through baptism opens his heart to receive God's manifold grace. The candidate likewise enlists for regular service as a soldier of the cross.

Such a view of the facts accords with the testimony of Saint Augustine, Bishop of Hippo. He is writing directly about the Trinity: " O Lord, our God, we believe in Thee, the Father and the Son and the Holy Ghost. For the Truth would not say, ' Go, baptize all nations in the Name of the Father and of the Son and of the Holy Ghost,' unless Thou wast a Trinity. Nor wouldest Thou, O Lord, bid us be baptized in the Name of Him who is not God."

In terms of today, the Trinity means that Christians worship the Father as God, the Son as God, and the Spirit as God. Although the Father stands first, he must be so among Persons each of whom is God. If all this must ever remain a mystery, it is one of light. A mystery, you remember, is a truth that we human beings could never discover for ourselves, but that we accept because it is revealed in the Scriptures, and confirmed in Christian experience.

The nature of the experience varies widely among different persons. With many of us the order of discovery follows that in the Apostolic Benediction, where the Lord Jesus comes first in time. Through the grace of Christ we become more and more thankful for the love of God the Father. Gradually we learn that all our blessings flow from him through the Holy Spirit.

With many a little boy the chief fact about religion is

Jesus. For a mature man the basic truth may be that of God the Father. In the heart of an elderly saint, who sits at the western window and waits for life's little day on earth to end, the most uplifting truth may be that of the Comforter. In view of these facts we should give thanks for the varieties of spiritual experience.

When a Christian has emerged from a Jewish background his creed may begin with God the Father. Such appears to have been the case with Heinrich Heine, the German poet and journalist. In terms of simple beauty, addressed to a growing boy, the poet tells how he came to know the truth about the blessed Trinity:

" Ah, my child, while I was yet a little boy, while I yet sat upon my mother's knee, I believed in God the Father, who rules up there in heaven, good and great; who created the beautiful earth, and the beautiful men and women thereon; who ordained for sun, moon, and stars their courses.

" When I got bigger, my child, I understood yet a great deal more than this, and comprehended, and grew intelligent; and now I believe on the beloved Son, who loved us and revealed love to us; and for His reward, as always happens, was crucified by the people.

" Now, when I am grown up, have read much, and have traveled much, my heart swells within me, and with my whole soul I believe in the Holy Ghost. The greatest miracles were of His working, and still greater miracles doth He even now work. He burst in sunder the oppressor's stronghold, and He cut in pieces the bondsman's yoke. He heals old death wounds, and renews the old right. All mankind are one race of noble equals before Him." " Glory be to the Father, and to the Son, and to the Holy Ghost! "

2. *The Trinity in Christian Experience.* Let us think more directly about the mercies that Christian worshipers ought to receive through the Apostolic Benediction. First of all, consider " the grace of the Lord Jesus Christ." Grace means the attractive goodness of God. Grace reveals the splendor of the indwelling light that makes him God. Such goodness shines out most clearly through the coming of our Redeemer and most strongly in his death upon the cross. Because he showed his love by his death for us there, we ought to rejoice in the grace that flows from Calvary.

Sometimes, alas, we forget that grace ought to be a matter of human experience as well as divine glory. When by faith the children of God receive the benediction, each of them ought to become more like Jesus. In the days of his flesh he was " full of grace and truth." In other words, the beauty of the Lord his God was upon him. The radiance of the unseen Father appeared in him whom we adore as " Fairest Lord Jesus." To be a Christian, therefore, must mean to be like him in the radiance of his ideal goodness. " Jesus takes up all the room in a believing heart."

The word " grace " likewise means the power that the Lord uses in supplying the needs of his followers, one by one. For instance, when the apostle pleaded that the thorn in his flesh might be removed, what was the answer? " My grace is sufficient for thee." According to the context, grace here means the strength of Christ Jesus made perfect in the weakness of his servant. In the power of that grace the apostle journeyed until his traveling days on earth were done. In short, eternity alone will reveal the wonders wrapped up in the words: " The grace of the Lord Jesus Christ."

A kindred blessing should come to believing hearts through the second portion of the benediction: " The Love of God." That means his love for us. Of course the minister's utterance of the appointed words can never increase God's concern for his children. He loved us ere we knew him, and he loves us still, to a degree that passes knowledge. Nevertheless, in the hour of worship, culminating with the benediction, there ought to be a new awareness of his love, and a fuller response to all its wonders.

Every hour of public worship should lead to what Robert Browning used to style " the soul's discovery of God." " What is it that I hunger for," he asks, " but for God? " Such a discovery of the Father in terms of love divine came to Helen Keller when she was ten years old. In an hour of perplexity she wrote a letter to her friend and hero, Phillips Brooks. Among other things she begged of him: " Please tell me something that you know about God." His message in response affords an example of the Father's love, about which he writes:

" Let me tell you how we come to know about our Heavenly Father. It is from the power of love in our own hearts. Love is at the soul of everything. God who is the greatest and happiest of all beings is the most loving too. All the love in our hearts comes from Him, as all the light in the flowers comes from the sun. The more we love, the nearer we are to God and His love . . . I love to tell you about God. But He will tell you about Himself by the love that He will put into your heart if you ask Him . . . Love is everything. If anybody asks you what God is, reply, ' God is love '! That is the beautiful answer the Bible gives."

Still a third blessing should come to God's children

through the Apostolic Benediction: " The communion
of the Holy Ghost." These familiar words mean that the
Spirit of the Lord goes with us on our way from Church,
and tarries with us as children of the Most High God.
The word " communion " literally means fellowship.
This in turn points to what we as Christians have in common through the Holy Spirit. What we hold in common
must be the grace of the Lord Jesus Christ and the love
of God the Father. There should likewise be Christian
fellowship among all the members of God's redeemed
family, both on earth and in heaven.

The Apostolic Church cherished such a spirit of
brotherly love. At Corinth, however, the congregation
became divided into cliques. Perhaps for that reason the
apostle closed his Second Epistle by invoking the communion of the Holy Spirit. In many a local Church today no gift from above should be more desired. If we love
not the brethren with whom we have prayed in the house
of the Lord, how do we know that we love the God whom
we can see only with the eyes of faith? On the other hand,
when the spirit of Christian love and forbearance spreads
out over the boundary lines between warring nations,
we can feel that the Church at large is beginning to be
one through the power of the Holy Spirit:

> " In Christ there is no East or West,
>   In Him no South or North;
> But one great fellowship of love
>   Throughout the whole wide earth."

At the close of the present hour you will receive the
Apostolic Benediction. By faith you will open your
hearts to " the manifold helpfulness of the Triune God."
Believing in God is important; receiving his favor is still
more vital. When by faith you accept the mercies that he

waits to bestow through the benediction, you will be ready to turn homeward. Then you can express in service what you have received in worship. Herein lies the meaning and the glory of the Trinity in Christian experience. The familiar words of the Apostolic Benediction actually convey divine power for all your needs. In the spirit of gratitude, therefore, bow down to receive the benediction:

" The grace of the Lord Jesus Christ, and the love of God, and the communion of the Holy Ghost, be with you all. Amen."

MOTHER'S DAY
Prov. 31:10–31; Rev. 21:1–7

THE PORTRAIT OF A GODLY MOTHER
" A woman that feareth the Lord, she shall be praised." — Prov. 31:30b.

THE closing verses of The Proverbs contain a full-length portrait of a godly mother. The Proverbs is the only book in the Bible written especially for young folk. In fact, the book is addressed mainly to one young man. It affords a practical theory of a planned life, with common-sense ways of living in a workaday world. At the end of the book a beautiful poem sings the praises of a godly mother. Such an upright woman, "not too . . . good for human nature's daily food," affords an object lesson of all the ideals and the duties set forth in the book of The Proverbs.

The poem takes the form of an acrostic. The Hebrew alphabet contains twenty-two letters. Hence the poem consists of that many parts, which we know as verses. Originally the aim must have been to encourage the growing boy in committing the words to memory. Ever afterward he would have in his heart an ideal of the one whom he ought some day to wed — " whoe'er she be, that not impossible she, that shall command my heart and me." In some other home, perhaps near by, a growing lass would learn by heart the same golden verses from The Proverbs. Then she would have ever in view a worthy ideal of what she ought to become: " A woman that feareth the Lord, she shall be praised." Here, then, we have a full-length portrait of a godly woman.

1. *The Charm of a Godly Woman*. In our Biblical word painting the subject of the study by the master artist is a woman of the Martha type. According to the Scriptures, the Lord Jesus loved both Martha and Mary. Both in religion and in life there should be room and a welcome for the sisters of Mary, gentle and mild, lovers of beauty and loyal to God. But at present we are to think about that larger throng, the daughters of Martha.

The heroine of our poem appears as a good woman of the Hebrew type. That sort of everyday saint has often arisen among the Scottish and the Dutch. The reason may be that such sturdy folk have reared their little ones on simple fare, often including porridge and proverbs. The woman before us works with zeal, and her strength never falters. Unlike many who bear heavy burdens today, she plans her routine tasks with wisdom and care. In fact, she serves as an object lesson of those vanishing virtues once known as Puritan: foresight, industry, and thrift.

Better still, this patron saint of old-time Hebrew women excels in the fine art of friendship. " She stretcheth out her hand to the poor." Sometimes we foolishly make sport of such frugal friends. We forget that they are always able and eager to reach out hands full of good things needful for God's suffering poor. Once again, " She openeth her mouth with wisdom; and in her tongue is the law of kindness." Such " sweetness and light " issue from a heart overflowing with love for the God who is " most wonderfully kind."

> " On that cheek, and o'er that brow,
>   So soft, so calm, so eloquent,
> The smiles that win, the tints that glow
>   But tell of days in goodness spent,
> A mind at peace with all below,
>   A heart whose love is innocent! "

2. *The Influence of a Godly Wife.* In Bible days the Hebrews believed in marriage. Rightly did they look upon it as the normal state of human beings here below. In it they found earth's nearest approach to heaven. By way of contrast think of the blight that falls upon many a home in days of war and reconstruction. Not only does war lead young folk to hasten or else postpone their wedding day. War also slays many a noble youth who would have gloried in being a husband and father. War likewise leaves unsought many a winsome maiden whom God must have meant to serve the common weal as a wife and mother in a Christian home.

Whether in war or peace, the woman who fears the Lord takes delight in being true to her marriage vows. " In plenty and in want; In joy and in sorrow; In sickness and in health; As long as we both do live," " the heart of her husband doth safely trust in her." Because she loves her God supremely, she is ever loyal to her husband. In every relation of their life together she wins the right to be called his helpmeet. Instead of adding to her husband's burdens, year after year she stands back of him as a sort of silent partner. " She will do him good and not evil all the days of his life." Through their love for each other, the two of them grow daily more like their God.

Largely because of her unseen influence, the husband may be a power among his fellow men. If so, he becomes " known in the gates, when he sitteth among the elders of the land." Little does he or anyone else ever dream that the inspiration and the strength for his life of service come from God through the influence of a quiet woman. She believes in her beloved. She expects from him everything good and high. This motif prevails in the charming domestic drama by Sir James M. Barrie, *What Every*

Woman Knows. What does she know? How to buckle
the armor on her husband's heart so that he stands up
day after day to win victories for the living God. Some
such vision must have been glowing in the eyes of
Wordsworth when he sang:

> " A perfect woman, nobly plann'd
> To warn, to comfort, and command;
> And yet a spirit still, and bright
> With something of angelic light."

By this time someone may be tempted to protest:
" Your good woman seems to be busy and troubled about
many things! Is she not a martyr to a mistaken sense of
duty? " No, not from the Biblical point of view. Her kind
of love never counts the cost of doing good. If ever she
were tempted to pity herself as a sort of household helper
she might recall the old-time essay by William C. Gan-
nett, under the title, " Blessed Be Drudgery ":

" We have to go, morning after morning, through
rain and through shine, through headache and through
heartache, to the appointed spot and to the given task.

" We have to stick to that work through eight or ten
hours, long after rest would be sweet. Good temper must
be kept with children, with neighbors, and perhaps with
servants, not seven times, but seventy times seven. The
besetting sin must be watched today and tomorrow and
every day. In short, without much matter where our
work may lie, it is because of the rut and the plod, the
grind and the humdrum, that we at last get laid the
foundations of character: attention and promptness,
accuracy and firmness, patience and self-denial, as well
as all the rest.

" Then beyond all books, all class-work, all special
opportunities of what I call my education, it is the drill

and pressure of my everyday work that is my best school-
master. My daily task, that is what chiefly educates me.
Yet, fool that I am, this pressure of my daily work I growl
at as my Drudgery! Blessed be Drudgery! "

3. *The Praises of a Godly Mother*. Most of all did the
ancient Hebrews believe in the bearing of children. This
belief also came from God. It still lies close to his heart.
Not only does he wish to be known as Father. He has
likewise filled the mother heart with a love like his own.
" As one whom his mother comforteth, so will I comfort
you." Hence the noblest tribute any mortal can bestow
on a woman in the home is to call her a godly mother.
Such a tribute may be one of her chief rewards, both on
earth and in glory.

" Her children arise up and call her blessed; her husband also, and he praiseth her." The rest of the poem
tells what these loved ones ought to say while she is with
them in the flesh. After her children are mature, and
have little ones of their own, her sons and daughters
should begin to appreciate their mother. They should
delight to join with their father in voicing her praises as
the uncrowned queen of the home. If they are wise they
understand that their mother loves and trusts each of her
children; that she prays and hopes for them one by one;
and that she lives and toils for them all together. Indeed,
she would gladly suffer and die to shield any of them
from harm.

In Kentucky years ago such a saintly mother presided
over a branch of the Breckinridge clan. From that home
went forth a group comprising the most illustrious sons
of the Bluegrass State, if not of the entire South. A
familiar legend says that after the four sons had become

famous, each in a different sphere, they all came home
to spend Christmas with their mother, then a widow.
As they sat together around the family board one of
them said to her, playfully: " Mother, you and father
were the noblest parents that growing boys could ever
know and love. But don't you think you were too strict
with us when we were small? "

" Robert," came the quick rejoinder, also with a smile,
" when you have reared four as fine sons as I have, you
can begin telling me how to raise children! " Well did
she know that the family tree should be judged by the
quality of its fruit.

Even the saintliest mother, however, cannot linger on
in the family circle forever. After she has gone home to
her God, the children of her heart's love still rise up and
call her blessed. Indeed, more than a few grown sons and
daughters calmly accept their mother's devotion as long
as she tarries with them in the flesh. At last, when she
has lain down to sleep at the end of her day on earth,
they find that they have had in their midst a dear one
much like God in heaven. Some such discovery has led
more than one worldly son or daughter to accept
mother's Saviour after she has gone home to rest. Perhaps this is what the apostle means by his unusual words
about being " baptized for the dead."

Once again I hear a protest. This one should be doubly
welcome, for it comes from an aged mother, who never
has spoken out in meeting. Surely she has a right to be
heard in the sanctuary! " Tell us," she whispers, " less
about mothers and more about God! " That is well
spoken. God alone can be the Source of all that is true
and strong, all that is lovely and enduring, in the heart
and life of any mother. Hence we should thank our God

for letting his love and mercy shine out on the world through the windows of a home where she is more than queen. Of such a dwelling place, full of light and life and love, LeBaron Russell Briggs teaches us to sing:

> "Thine is the strong and solemn glow,
> Thine is the sweet abounding grace,
> Of her whose love, through weal and woe,
> Lights her transcendent face.
> Where hope is high and thought is free,
> Where life is brave and death is true,
> Where duty unrelenting leads
> To tasks of pain forever new,
> The heart that triumphs while it bleeds,
> Mother, thy face we see."

This would be a fitting stage for a word of prayer. In it everyone should accept anew the mercies that come from God through mother's love. Afterward we all could sing a parting hymn. Then the minister would pronounce the benediction of God's light and peace. On the homeward way one after another might exclaim: " I am truly grateful for my mother and her undying love! "

All that has its worthy place, but still God requires more. He has no patience with sentimentality. How can he bless a man or a woman who receives but never shares? The Lord's standard for living at home is clear: " Unto whomsoever much is given, of him shall be much required." Here and now he wishes each of you to ask: " Am I worthy of my mother's love? Am I walking in her footsteps, even as she followed the Master? In days to come will my children and children's children rise up and call me blessed? "

As we bow in silent prayer let each of us give himself anew into the hands of God, for Christian love and service in the home.

BACCALAUREATE SUNDAY
Micah 6:1–8; Matt. 7:13–27

THE RELIGION OF A MODERN MAN

*" He hath shewed thee, O man, what is good;
and what does the Lord require of thee, but to do
justly, and to love mercy, and to walk humbly
with thy God? " — Micah 6:8.*

THESE words show the spirit of a man's religion. For
many reasons no one has ever been able to define the
term " religion." It reaches up as high as heaven and
stretches out over all the earth. However, if you think
of religion as it relates to a single person, especially yourself, you can reduce the matter to its lowest common
denominator. When you compare your findings with
the words of the prophet, you will see that he has put
into a few simple words the essence of religion for a
modern man.

At the Library of Congress in Washington, D.C., there
stands in the main reading room a statue entitled
Religion. Over the statue hangs a plaque with an inscription chosen by former President Charles W. Eliot
of Harvard. Before the present building was formally
opened in 1897, those in charge requested him to phrase
the various mottoes. When he came to the statue in honor
of religion, instead of employing words of his own, as a
modern man he preferred to borrow the terms of our
text: " What doth the Lord require of thee, but to do
justly, and to love mercy, and to walk humbly with
thy God? "

This working description of a man's religion has three
emphases.

1. *The Doing of Justice*. This is basic. In the opening words of the text, as in each of the parts that follow, much depends upon the verb. The Lord requires that a man do justly. God can never rest content with one who simply admires and praises this virtue in others. The voice of our King summons each of us to action. From this point of view a man's religion calls for translating lofty ideals into workaday living. "Not everyone that saith to me, Lord, Lord, shall enter into the kingdom of heaven; but he that doeth the will of my Father."

To do justly means that a man gets right with God as his Father; keeps right with other people, one by one; and stays right within himself. As William James used to say, to be religious means that a man should be consciously "right, superior, and happy." Instead of thinking about duty as "the Stern Daughter of the Voice of God," one should find the doing of justice a source of increasing delight.

While a man is young he may find it hard to form habits of doing justly. He may deem it irksome always to be asking whether a certain course is right or wrong. But in later years the one who has made it a rule to follow his conscience should enjoy an unfailing succession of wholesome memories. According to the autobiography of the late William Lyon Phelps, beloved professor at Yale, the happiest man on earth is the one who cherishes the most interesting thoughts. Therefore if you wish to prepare for a peaceful old age, begin now to do justly: "Remember now thy Creator in the days of thy youth."

In a time when the world has been at war everyone should likewise think of justice as it concerns the nations. In a sense a man's righteousness, with his charity, begins at home. The place to start doing justice is where you live and work day after day. But in a man's prayers and through his influence he should also seek for the triumph of justice throughout the earth. Both in the home community and in China, as well as among the Japanese who have been corralled in Arizona and the outcastes of distant India, the Christian man should long to see justice enthroned. For such world righteousness many a strong young soldier has made the supreme sacrifice.

Today God is calling for men and women able to translate lofty idealism into practical service. As long as justice seems to be only an abstraction, it can influence the spirit of our age little more than the snow on the Himalayas affects the heat of southern India. When shall we idealistic Americans learn that justice is to be done for colored folk as well as white, and that the doing rests partly with each of us? Among all the needs of a world that has grown desperate, first of all our times demand the sort of God who reveals himself through men as doers of righteousness.

Under God, the most vital fact about our nation is the quality of its manhood. In Greece during the fourth century, B.C., the ruler of Sparta was Agesilaus II. A visitor once asked him why, among all the city states of Greece, Sparta alone had erected no walls for defense. The king pointed to his young men of war, who stood in array as for battle. Then he said, " Sir, there are the walls of Sparta, and every man a brick."

In order to be used in the building of a better world, a man needs to be right with God. In religion and in life, justice ought to serve as the basic fact. The man in view also needs to be right with his neighbors and friends; that is, with every person whose life he should touch. Meanwhile he himself ought to be a good brick. Even the Almighty cannot build up the City of God with bricks that are not sound at heart. All this and more the man of today should mean when he says to himself, " What doth the Lord require of thee but to do justly? "

2. *The Love of Kindness.* In our working description of a man's religion this is a still more vital quality. Of course justice must ever come first. It serves as the foundation rock on which a man builds the house where he plans to dwell with his wife and children. But a life full of justice without mercy would be as bleak and cold as an unheated basement in December. For instance, consider Old Scrooge in *A Christmas Carol,* by Charles Dickens; Silas Marner in the novel under that name, written by George Eliot; or dour old Davie Deans in *The Heart of Midlothian,* by Sir Walter Scott. On the other hand, each of those novels shows by contrast the beauty of kindness that is based on justice. Where in all literature, for instance, can you see a more worthy young woman than Scott's Jeanie Deans? She took delight in doing justice and in loving mercy.

" What doth the Lord require of thee but . . . to love mercy? " Here again the verb shares honors with the noun. Mercy is another name for loving-kindness. That in turn should mean to be like God. He performs acts of justice; he takes delight in deeds of mercy. To show how much he loves to be kind, he has made his mercy known in Christ and the cross. Even when our Lord was dying, he breathed out words of loving-kindness, for both friend and foe. Likewise when he spoke about the coming Judgment Day he set up as a standard the love of mercy like his own: " Inasmuch as ye have done it unto one of the least of these my brethren, ye have done it unto me." According to such a lofty ideal, what is your own spiritual stature? The question is voiced by Edwin Markham in his poem, " If He Should Come ":

> " If Jesus should tramp the streets tonight,
>   Storm-beaten and hungry for bread,
>   Seeking a room and a candle light,
>   And a clean though humble bed,
>   Who would welcome the Workman in,
>   Though He came with panting breath,
>   His hands all bruised and His garments thin —
>   This Workman from Nazareth? "

For a living example of one who strove to fulfill the law of justice, and found his joy in being kind, turn to Abraham Lincoln. Such a spirit shines out especially from his Second Inaugural Address and from his letter to Mrs. Bixby. His kindness to her, a total stranger, should mean all the more when we remember that his own heart was broken because death had recently taken his favorite son, little Tad.

" I have been shown in the files of the War Department a statement that you are the mother of five sons who have died gloriously on the field of battle. . . . I cannot refrain from tendering the consolation that may be found in the thanks of the Republic they died to save. I pray that the Heavenly Father may assuage the anguish of your bereavement and leave you only the cherished memories of the loved and lost, and the solemn pride that must be yours to have laid so costly a sacrifice upon the altar of freedom."

Now that the world is facing the need of reconstruction, our religion calls for both justice and mercy or, rather, for mercy on the basis of justice. In our own history as a nation the spirit of tolerance and forgiveness of erstwhile enemies came to its fullness in two strong men during a war that might have bred hatred in their high places. Both in Robert E. Lee and in Abraham Lincoln, as well as in Queen Victoria across the ocean, the peoples of the English-speaking world have long been able to see object lessons of how to blend devotion to conscience with love of kindness. Would that such a spirit might also have prevailed throughout our days of " Reconstruction "!

In recent years the spirit of loyalty to justice and mercy, especially mercy, has breathed through all the public utterances of two Christians who have had abundant reason to hate the invading foe. If ever a land has been overrun and a people downtrodden, without provocation or excuse, that country has been China. If ever innocent people have suffered indignities too awful for human speech, those have been the followers of General and Madame Chiang Kai-shek. Nevertheless, in his prayers at the family altar, as reported by a visitor from Canada, the generalissimo besought the Almighty to keep him and his followers from hating the Japanese people. He even implored God to bless the men who had been dropping bombs on defenseless women and children, with no military objective in view. Would that such a spirit of magnanimity might prevail in the hearts of outraged peoples everywhere today! Christ still says, " Love your enemies "!

3. *The Spirit of Humility*. This third element seems the most amazing. " What doth the Lord require of thee but . . . to walk humbly with thy God? " When justice

undergirds all a man's actions, he may easily become proud. Such a spirit of haughtiness marked many of the Pharisees. The man who does his full duty, and then goes the second mile in the way of mercy, may be tempted to feel better than his neighbors. If there were any way of setting up such a Gallup Poll, we might discover many strong men who strive to be just; a smaller number who succeed in being just and kind; but only a handful who are able to blend these qualities with the spirit of meekness.

Perhaps because of its rarity, this virtue makes a strong appeal to many a modern man. During World War I, no religious leader addressed more men in uniform than did Fred B. Smith. After the servicemen had returned to their homes he reported that the " doughboy " or the " gob," as well as the " leatherneck," required of his hero three qualities: courage, kindness, and humility. Negatively, according to this friendly observer, the men in the ranks looked down on the officer who was cowardly, mean, or boastful. Here is one of many tokens that you can trust the ideals of the average man.

What, then, does the prophet mean by humility? Does it not set forth the spirit of the man who depends on the Lord? The text says that the ideal man walks with God. To walk with him means to know him and to love him, to be like him and to keep moving forward, step by step, in doing what pleases him. " Can two walk together, except they be agreed? " Such a manly religion provides no room for the cringing, fawning flattery of a Uriah Heep, who goes about boasting of what he styles his " 'umility." Rather does the spirit of our text call for robust self-respect, because a man is accounted wor-

thy to be a friend of the King. However, the one who is
truly meek never presumes on his friendship with Christ.

To be humble also means that a man is quick to dis-
cern goodness in other people, one by one. As an example, think of that Christian gentleman and poet,
Robert Browning. For years few of the critics could see
in his verses aught of beauty or worth, and many poets
failed to sense the power of his rugged lines. Nevertheless, Browning spoke well of almost every poet then at
work in England. Could there be a more searching test
of love for one's fellow men?

When a man puts God first, and others second, he
thinks of himself modestly. In fact, he may become so
busily engaged in doing right, in loving mercy, and in
walking humbly with God, that he seldom turns his
thoughts in on self. If he does so, occasionally, it is to
regret that he falls short of his ideals. " A man's reach
should exceed his grasp, or what's a heaven for? "

A perfect blending of justice, kindness, and humility
appears only in the earthly life of our Lord. Seldom does
he stand out more attractively than in Thorvaldsen's
statue, *The Christus.* The original work of art belongs
in Copenhagen, but an exact copy stands within the main
entrance of the Johns Hopkins Hospital at Baltimore.
The inscription tells why every Christian doctor or
nurse ought to revere the Beloved Physician: " Come
unto me, all ye that labour and are heaven laden, and I
will give you rest."

In the spirit of these beautiful words, listen again to
our text: " He hath shewed thee, O man, what is good;
and what doth the Lord require of thee, but to do justly,
to love mercy, and to walk humbly with thy God? " If

that is what it means to live as a child of the heavenly Father, how do you personally measure up to the standard? Surely the response of many a heart must be a confession of failure:

O Lord our God, in the light of this Hebrew ideal I am ashamed and sorry. Much have I striven to do justly, to love mercy, and to walk humbly with my God. But again and again have I fallen short. Now I see that I must no longer depend on myself. Here, then, I kneel, to find pardon, cleansing, and peace. Take me, O Lord, just as I am; make me what I ought to become. Then use me in helping others, one by one, to seek the sort of religion that makes a man just, moves him to be kind, and keeps him humble, all for the sake of Jesus Christ, our Lord. Amen.

CHILDREN'S DAY

Deut. 6:4–9; Matt. 18:1–14

THE HERITAGE OF OUR CHILDREN
" The children ought not to lay up for the parents, but the parents for the children." — II Cor. 12:14d.

WHAT are you laying up for your children? The query is in line with this text from Saint Paul. He never had little ones of his own. But, like many another childless minister, the apostle loved a host of human beings. He looked on them all as his children. In the letter before us he is explaining to his friends at Corinth how they ought to live in a worldly city. In the words surrounding our text he is making clear his personal attitude towards money. He shows that he loves people more than things, and that he enjoys giving far more than getting. He takes delight in giving himself and his heart's love. What a model for Christian parents! Surely we all are concerned about the heritage of our children.

The present sermon, like many another, has grown out of a personal experience. In southern Ohio one week I visited six counties known afar for the fertility of their soil. At each successive county seat I spoke to a group of men and women who were concerned about the welfare of boys and girls. Before starting out on the circuit, I wrote to a leading citizen of each town and asked him to tell me frankly what the people of his community were doing to make the men and women of tomorrow more than worthy of their parents.

One of the replies ran as follows: " Most of the fathers and mothers in this county seem to be intent on laying up money; they wish to leave each child a good house; they are working hard so as to hand over large investments." The brother who sent me that report may have been a victim of what Mr. Wendell Willkie terms " corrosive, cynical pessimism." Even so, the account sets off in sharp relief the contrast between the Biblical ideal of life and the pagan philosophy of things. From the Christian point of view, as set forth by the Apostle Paul, let us consider the heritage of our sons and daughters: " The children ought not to lay up for the parents, but the parents for the children." What should we lay up, and how?

1. *The Heritage of Happy Memories.* According to the Christian view of life, it is better by far to leave the children happy memories than hoards of money. Under God, the usefulness of your sons and daughters in years to come may depend largely upon their recollections of early childhood. In fact, the magic spell of a happy home begins to work on a little heart long before the age of memory. That is why a daughter in our family circle started to pray aloud with her baby as soon as he was born. Such lofty idealism comes from a book long famous. In his *Christian Nurture* Horace Bushnell says: " Let every Christian father and mother understand, when their child is three years old, that they have done more than half of all they will ever do for his character."

Testimony of a rather different sort issues from that thought-provoking novel, *The Brothers Karamazov,* by Feodor Dostoevski: " There is nothing stronger and more wholesome for life in the future than some good memory, especially a memory of childhood and home. . . . Some good, sacred memory is perhaps the best education. If a man carries many such memories with him into life, he is safe to the end of his days. If one has only a single good memory left in one's heart, even that may sometimes be the means of saving one's soul. That lone memory may keep one from some great evil."

Many of life's most joyful recollections ought to cluster round the thought of mother. Provided she is true to her God, the chief privilege of a mother may be that of spreading sunshine. Since religion is more easily caught than taught, she can influence her little ones most surely by letting her light shine out amid a happy home. It seems to have been so with the mothers of two Presidents, who differed widely and still were friends. On the evening of the day when Grover Cleveland finally left the White House he wrote: " I have had a long talk with President McKinley. He is an honest, sincere, and serious man. I feel that he is going to do his best to give the country a good administration. I envied him today only one thing, the presence of his mother at his Inauguration."

Happy memories should also be associated with the father. Too lightly do we assume that he should leave to the mother all the privileges of shedding sunshine into little hearts and lives. In her autobiography, *Twenty Years at Hull-House,* Jane Addams shows that she almost worshiped her father. As a little girl with a physical handicap, she supposed that her father must feel ashamed of such a daughter. But one day she discovered indirectly that he loved her all the more because of her infirmity. Ever afterward life to her meant trying to measure up to the loving expectations of her father. Fortunately, a father need not be famous in order to possess a store of such joyous recollections. Here are excerpts from a letter written by a missionary wife to her father. He was a man past middle age, and by no means a pauper. But he took more delight in this one letter than in all his worldly goods:

" How thankful I am for you and for all the blessed memories of you! I am grateful that you have always been my good friend and my best beau; that you have taken me with you in your work and your play. Body, mind, and soul I owe you a debt that I can never repay, except by being the very best, most loving, and most sympathetic mother. I trust that I shall succeed as you have done. Being in touch with the Source of your success, I know that I shall succeed."

In a home with the right sort of father and mother there are sure to be happy memories. Many of these joyous recollections should have to do with religion. In the experience of a growing child the spirit of Christianity calls for a blending of love, joy, and serenity. In the words of grace before the family meal; in the few minutes of worship as a household, after the morning and the evening repast; above all, in the bedtime stories and the words of prayer before the good-night kiss, the dominant note should be that of joy. Such a home affords an object lesson of the heaven where some day the children of God are to be " lost in wonder, love, and praise." This kind of blessed hope led Henry van Dyke to sing about " The Builders ":

> " O Thou whose boundless love bestows
>   The joy of earth, the hope of Heaven,
> And whose uncharted mercy flows
>   O'er all the blessings Thou hast given;
> Thou by whose light alone we see;
> And by whose truth our souls set free
>   Are made imperishably strong;
> Hear Thou the solemn music of our song."

2. *The Heritage of Good Habits.* It is wiser to lay up for the children a store of good habits than to give each of them a grand house. The possession of a worthy home may be a token of God's favor; but for most of us mortals that comes towards the middle years of life, if ever at all on earth. Worthy habits, on the other hand, ought to mark the early years of our sons and daughters, as well as of our grandchildren. Under God, their usefulness in time to come will depend largely on the habit systems they are building up today. That is the teaching of both religion and psychology. In fact, " the laws of habit," as set forth by William James, afford an up-to-date commentary on parts of the letter written by the most practical of all the apostles.

First among good habits must stand obedience. The Fifth Commandment still holds: " Honour thy father and thy mother." To honor means to obey, in the spirit of love. If our sons and daughters are later to excel as employees or employers, as private citizens or leaders of others, their basic need will be that of discipline, which begins with obedience. Sometimes the teen-age boy learns to obey after he has gone from home, perhaps to war. But the experience of John Wesley and his brother Charles shows that infancy is the ideal time for learning to obey. Would that every family with growing children might have such a godly mother as Susanna Wesley, and such an expert in loving discipline!

In the beauty of life's morning little boys and girls should be forming still other old-fashioned habits. Among them stand out courtesy, chivalry, and hospitality. If these ways of living are to sit gracefully upon the grown man or woman, the habits must be formed early in life, the sooner the better. In certain homes, not least in the South, it used to be expected that the wee

boy would become a Christian gentleman, and that the
tiny girl would grow into a gentlewoman, worthy to become the wife of a noble man, the mother of his children,
and the grandmother of his grandchildren. With such
training of little ones God is well pleased, for he is our
Father.

Highest of all among worthy habits stands reverence.
Apart from the home, the best place to develop this
virtue is the sanctuary. Such counsel appears in a wise
little book, *What You Owe Your Child,* by Dean Willard
L. Sperry of Harvard. Writing especially to young
mothers, he insists that for any growing boy or girl the
most vital hour of all the week is the time of public
worship. There the child should sit in the family pew
with father and mother. Thus early in life every boy or
girl should form the habit of enthusiastic attendance at
Church. On the other hand, we who are responsible for
public worship ought to lead aright. Then the little boy
can bow down as soon as he enters the sanctuary and
whisper the words that he uses back home at the dinner
table: " Lord, make us grateful for what we are about
to receive."

Thus far no one has invented any modern substitute
for the family pew as a training school in reverence.
Such testimony comes indirectly from the late Walter Rauschenbusch. Much as he felt concerned about
" Christianity and the social crisis," he never lost sight
of the one little boy or girl whom Jesus loved. The current biographer says that as a wee lad Walter attended
his father's Church every Lord's Day. There the child
was impressed most of all by the Communion service
and the ordinance of baptism. Throughout a busy life
he continued to cherish the habit of reverence in the

house of God. Hence Rauschenbusch could write his most praiseworthy book, *Prayers of the Social Awakening.* Should there not be a spiritual awakening in the heart of every little boy or girl?

Similar testimony comes from Dr. Albert Schweitzer. He writes about attending Church with his parents at Günsbach: "From the services in which I joined as a child I have taken into life a feeling for what is solemn, and a need for quiet and self-recollection, without which I cannot realize the meaning of my life. I cannot therefore support the opinion of those who would not let children take part in grown-up people's services till they to some extent understand. The important thing is not that they shall understand but that they shall feel something of what is serious and solemn. The fact that the child sees his elders full of devotion, and has to feel something of their devotion himself — that is what gives the service its meaning for him."

To these old-fashioned ideas about the training of children some of our ablest leaders are beginning to return. After long years of dealing with adults at Hull House, Jane Addams concluded that the surest way to reach human beings is to start with children. More recently Kagawa was striving to reclaim outcasts in the city slums of Japan. A friend suggested that it would be better to begin with the boys and girls. Kagawa is said to have replied that he was unwilling to wait until they had grown up so that he could see the fruits of his toil.

After he had labored among fallen men and women for a quarter of a century, Kagawa changed his mind: "I must confess that I made a serious mistake. If I had put more energy into the winning of children for Christ

I should probably have been more successful. I was too impatient to wait ten or fifteen years for them to become adults." God grant that no parent here shall ever be forced to make such a humble confession about the children now at home. Today is the time to reach the hearts of little boys and girls in the name of Jesus. Lead them now to form the habit of honoring him.

3. *The Heritage of Lofty Ideals.* It is more Christian to leave grown children with lofty ideals than with large investments. We have been thinking about character-building in terms of growing importance. To lay up for your children a store of happy memories ought to make home seem like heaven. To train them in worthy habits should prepare them for active membership in God's family here on earth. To send them forth with lofty ideals should lead them close to the heart of the Saviour. When at the age of twelve, or perhaps a little later, they put in his hands the keeping of their hearts and lives, they will be ready for training as good soldiers of Jesus Christ. Memories, habits, ideals! The best of the three is the heritage of lofty ideals. To that inheritance let us now turn.

Ideals have to do with the future. If they are Christian they include at least a glimpse of the life everlasting. But for a little boy or girl ideals should relate to things that can be seen here and now. One of the most vital should concern the home. There from the day of his birth the growing lad should be surrounded with love, joy, and peace. Erelong he should begin to dream of the place where someday he will dwell as husband and father. In the heart of almost every little boy the Lord plants the desire to build a home for human beings. In that dreamland household he should look forward to being a father much like God.

> " Who is the happy husband? He
> Who, scanning his unwedded life,
> Thanks heaven, with a conscience free,
> 'Twas faithful to his wife."

The ideals of a wee girl may also prove uplifting. With her the normal desire should be to play with dolls. A little later she may want to mother the weak and helpless. In the years following World War II she may be forced to go through life without knowing the joys of a wife and mother. Nevertheless, her heart should be filled with love for little children. When at last she lies down to sleep at the end of a long and busy day on earth, her friends near and far should thank God for the ideals of God's gentlewoman. Over in Africa when Mary Slessor came to the close of her seventy years, most of it spent in helping natives to find peace and joy through Jesus as Lord, those childlike folk exclaimed, " Everybody's mother is dead! "

When lofty ideals are born of God they do not always lead the growing boy whither he expects to go. Out of his own experience Frederick W. Robertson was led to preach one of his most moving sermons, " The Illusiveness of Life." Throughout his early years, until he became twenty-one, he had set his heart on becoming a soldier like his father and others in the family circle. Even after the young man was ordained as a minister of the Gospel, at heart he remained a soldier. To his calling in the Church he brought brilliant gifts and disciplined powers, which would have insured his rapid advancement as an officer in Her Majesty's Army. When he laid down his life at the early age of thirty-seven, the Church began to discover that he had been the foremost preacher of his day. After the lapse of almost a hundred years his *Sermons Preached at Brighton* have been reprinted in popular form. Thus they serve as object lessons showing how God blesses the lofty ideals of a boy. Ofttimes they lead him to become a power among men in a field of which he has never dreamed.

All these God-given ideals — such as home-building, usefulness, and Christian influence — belong together. From one point of view any such heavenly vision shines like the star that led the Magi to the Babe of Bethlehem. However, such guidance from above may not lead to what we narrowly speak of as " Christian service." Not every girl ought to become an unmarried missionary. Not every boy should grow up to serve God as a busy pastor. For this reason, if for no other, the fond parent should never suggest what lifework the son or daughter ought to choose as a means of serving God and men. Rather should it be the father's and mother's joy to send the young folk forth with the sort of ideals that God can use in leading them one by one as he did with Abraham of old: " By faith . . . he went out, not knowing whither."

Who would ever dream, for instance, of serving God as a comedian? Yet for years that was the role of Harry Lauder. Especially after he gave up his son in World War I, Sir Harry used wholesome fun in bringing solace to many a broken heart. When someone inquired about his practical philosophy of life, the Christian comedian pondered over the matter for a while. Then he spoke in terms of the old village lamplighter. In the evening after the boy Harry had finished his day's work down in the mines he used to sit out on the front porch and watch his old friend light one gas lamp after another. When he had completed his rounds, the lamplighter would go to his home and lie down to sleep. Through the long hours of darkness those lights that he had caused to burn would guide one person after another safely to his home. In like manner, said the Scottish comedian, every Christian should know the joy of starting other lives to burning and shining for God. The best time to do that is in their childhood, or else in youth.

Many a pastor has discovered that the surest way to win recruits for Christ's army is to begin with boys and girls. As he gains more experience he also meets with a glad response from their fathers and mothers. When little ones are growing up in a home not Christian, young parents soon feel the need of a power higher than their own. Because of their God-given love for the little children, more than a few parents become loyal followers of Christ and active members of the home Church. " A little child shall lead them." In the name of the Father God, therefore, I implore you now to become a Christian for your child's sake.

As a father or mother, you are engaged in the most Godlike calling on earth. The Almighty himself has bidden you train the little ones for his service. He is waiting now to lead and bless as you lay up for your children an increasing store of happy memories, good habits, and lofty ideals. But before you can begin to do so, you need to be much like God. Father of a growing son, have you considered the need of becoming a strong Christian for your boy's sake? Mother of a little girl, have you given yourself to Jesus for your daughter's sake? Here and now, through love for that child, God is leading you close to the heart of Christ.

INSTALLATION SERVICE
II Cor. 4:1–18

THE TREASURE IN EARTHEN VESSELS
" We have this treasure in earthern vessels." — II Cor. 4:7.

WHAT a strange text for an installation service! The words bring to view a row of old cracked crocks. How cheap! How ugly! How commonplace! When a young minister stands on the threshold of his lifework, with all its promise and glory spread out before him, his friends and well-wishers think of his ministry in terms of silver and gold, as well as precious stones. But here the ablest of Christian clergymen writes about work for God in terms of old cracked crocks! What does he mean?

How can we translate the glowing imagery of the apostle into the colder prose of our time? Let us say that the heavenly treasure sets forth divine power, and that the earthen vessels symbolize human weakness. According to the ways of God, divine power works through human weakness. Herein lies the secret of Christian radiance, both for the minister and for the local Church. Heavenly treasure in earthen vessels!

The apostle must be inspired. Not otherwise would he dare to speak of himself and a beloved congregation as earthen vessels. Being led of the Spirit, Paul appeals to the eye of the soul. He himself has long been a seer. Since his heart is " strangely warmed," as well as moved, his written words almost sing. He loves to tell about " the light of the knowledge of the glory of God in the face of Jesus Christ." Such is the heavenly treasure we should have in our earthen vessels.

By the treasure Paul means the Gospel of the blessed God. What the apostle writes about the heavenly treasure far surpasses what he tells about the earthen vessels. If we are to make the most of our earthen vessels we must form the habit of thinking much about the treasure within. But before we can learn what Paul has in mind about the treasure we must think of those earthen jars. Hence we should begin, not with light that streams from heaven, but with crocks made out of common clay.

1. *Earthen Vessels Symbolize Human Weakness.* The apostle is writing about himself and the Church at Corinth. As we think together about cheap cracked crocks, let each of us refer the figure to himself and the congregation that he loves more than aught in the world, except his home. That too must be an earthen vessel.

Even the best of human beings may look like an old cracked crock. That seems to have been the case with the apostle. To us he serves as an ideal. If there were need of a Pope, the majority of us would vote for Saint Paul. Indeed, he sometimes threatens to overshadow Christ. But if Paul could hear our words of fulsome praise he would protest with all his might: " No, no, I too am a man! In sooth, I am only an old cracked crock! "

The apostle may refer to his body. He lived in the Mediterranean world, where the culture came from Greece. Well did he know that the Greeks of his day almost worshiped the beauty of the human body. He was writing to the " saints " in a Grecian city noted for the splendor of its " Corinthian Games." All the while, if only by way of contrast with athletes, he must have been thinking of his own warped body.

Elsewhere the apostle speaks about his physical ap-

pearance as " contemptible." His bodily make-up seems
to have been so ludicrous that the urchins would sneer
as he walked down the street, " There goes that ugly
little Jew! " His physical strength appears to have been
limited. He also suffered from a malady that he described
as " a thorn in the flesh." Whatever its nature — whether
trouble with his eyes, malaria, or epilepsy — that dis-
order in his body must have been chronic. Surely it was
painful, if not excruciating. At times it threatened to
thwart his work for Christ and the Church.

To such physical handicaps he had to add the fact of
advancing years. Since he dwelt in a world that almost
worshiped the prowess of young athletes, the apostle
may have felt half guilty for growing old. The Church
still counts that offense almost unpardonable in a minister. He was beginning to grow frail. As " Paul the
aged " he knew that the earthen vessel would become
more and more fragile. Some day the pitcher would be
broken at the fountain. In short, he knew that he had
to die. Nevertheless, his heart was full of peace to overflowing. Did he not know that he had almost completed
the work set before him by his God?

Such a train of thought need cause no gloom. In 1829,
at the age of sixty-two, John Quincy Adams retired from
the Presidency of the United States. A year later he was
elected to serve in the House of Representatives. There
he spent his last eighteen years, which seem to have been
the most fruitful portion of his long career. One day not
long before his death, he was walking down Pennsylvania Avenue. There he met two friends. When they
stopped to ask about his health, the old gentleman replied: " I am well, thank you, but I have received notice
that some of these days I must move. This house in which

I have made my home for more than eighty years is getting sadly out of repair. The Owner informs me that I must bid my neighbors and friends adieu. But I am well! God bless you! "

Even the noblest of God's children on earth must " have this treasure in earthen vessels." The truth before us also applies to the local Church. The best of human institutions must fall far short of perfection. In the midst of a wicked city the gathering of the saints at Corinth may have seemed to its members almost ideal. But to the Apostle Paul that congregation was an earthen vessel. The same principle applies to the Church where we are now assembled. Doubtless the incoming minister has dreamed of an ideal parish. But soon or late he will discover that the only perfect congregation is in the New Jerusalem. Here on earth the glory of the Gospel must shine out through the windows of a Church with all sorts of handicaps and limitations, not to speak of imperfections and sins.

Thus we might look at still other institutions that a pastor finds full of flaws. One of them is the minister's home, where imperfect Christians learn the meaning of " forbearing one another in love." Another earthen vessel is the public school, where he may think of little boys and girls as basking in light from the throne of God. As he goes about among men and women he discovers that every one of them lives and works amid conditions by no means ideal. From day to day as he intercedes for his country he finds that it falls far below the standards set up by the fathers. If he follows this train of thought much farther he may become blue. Then he may wonder how God can use and bless such old cracked crocks.

In some dark hour the young idealist will awake to

the fact that he and his beloved Church are vessels of earth. Then he may find solace in the legend about an old rabbi, who served as the chief adviser of the king. One day the rabbi was conversing with the king's daughter, a maiden fair to the outer view, clad in beauty like the morning star. Perhaps for this reason she did not look with favor on the aged rabbi. " When my father might have about him young men, brilliant and handsome," she said with a sneer, " why does he choose as chief adviser a thing like you? "

Not wishing to offend her royal highness, the rabbi made answer: " Pardon me, Princess; why does your father keep the royal wine in jars of earth, and not in vessels of silver? " Indignantly she informed the rabbi that he was mistaken. But soon she discovered that he had spoken aright. So she wheedled her father into having the liquid treasure poured into bowls of silver. There the wine quickly began to turn sour. Then the rabbi asked the Princess: " Have you never noticed that God puts his choicest treasure in earthen crocks, that the vessels may call no attention away from the treasure? "

2. *The Heavenly Treasure Must Be a Token of Divine Power.* In other words, God does his best work through men and women far from perfect, and through institutions far from perfect. At present we are concerned only with the Church and the minister. Let us see how the principle applies to the Church. Then we can ask how the truth concerns the pastor.

A glance over the history of the Church will show that God does his best work through religious institutions by no means ideal. For example, think of the Old Testament Church. When did it ever enjoy a golden age? Perhaps in the era of King David. Who would ever dream of calling the Church of that day ideal? From any point of view it was only an earthen vessel. Still it contained a heavenly treasure. Out from that Hebrew Church came the Bible, the Lord Jesus, and the Gospel of the Kingdom.

Turn with me now to the New Testament Church. When did it glow with light from heaven? Never more than on the Day of Pentecost, when the saints appear to have been assembled in the upper room. Everyone who has visited the " upper room " in Jerusalem can bear witness that the scene of the Pentecostal outpouring must have been far from imposing. Of course, few scholars suppose that the present " upper room " was standing in the Holy City when the hundred and twenty disciples gathered to pray for the Holy Spirit. But everyone who knows the facts about Jerusalem in the days of the apostles will agree that the original upper room must have displayed no outward grandeur.

In the eyes of the Eastern world that upper room must have seemed like an earthen vessel. Even so, in the providence of God out from that humble source came the Christian Church. To that upper room we Christians must look for the fountainhead of our worship, our evangelism, and our missions. In like manner, hosts of Wesleyans across the sea, and of Methodists here at home, look back to a lowly shrine in Aldersgate Street, London. There on May 27, 1738, the heart of John Wesley was " strangely warmed." Who would ever have supposed that out from an earthen vessel could stream such floods of enduring light?

Once again, let us consider the Mediterranean world.

In recent days of war our sons have learned to think of Greek architecture in terms of classic beauty, of Roman buildings for magnitude, and of Mohammedan mosques because of magnificence. For example, take the ruins of the Parthenon in Athens, and of the Roman temples at Baalbek. Also think of the Blue Mosque and Saint Sophia at Istanbul. After viewing such scenes of splendor consider the humble quarters of the American Mission in Cairo. Under God, however, the hope for the Near East rests not in its vast mosques, with no indwelling light, but in humble meeting places on which men look down as earthen vessels. Out from those lowly houses of worship there streams " the light of the knowledge of the glory of God in the face of Jesus Christ."

The same principle of treasure in earthen vessels applies to men and women, one by one. God chooses to do his work through human beings full of faults and shortcomings. For example, think of bodily appearance. Among all our preachers in the English-speaking world, who has been more homely, and more powerful, than Charles Haddon Spurgeon or Bishop Matthew Simpson? Among earth's rulers, who has been more uncomely, and more revered, than Abraham Lincoln or Queen Victoria? In bodily strength who has been more frail, and more used of God, than Alice Freeman Palmer or Elizabeth Barrett Browning? " God hath chosen the weak things of the world to confound the things that are mighty."

Sometimes the physical handicap seems to be serious. In 1652, when John Milton was past forty-three years of age, he became blind. After that he gave the world his three masterpieces: *Paradise Lost, Paradise Regained,* and *Samson Agonistes.* In 1660, John Bunyan was shut up in Bedford Jail. There he tarried, except for brief

intervals, through twelve long years. During his first imprisonment he wrote his autobiography, *Grace Abounding*. Before he was finally set free he had largely composed his masterpiece, *The Pilgrim's Progress*. What
heavenly light to stream from earthen vessels!

In 1882, a little Alabama girl scarcely two years old
suffered an attack of scarlet fever. Thus she lost the
sense of sight, of smell, and of hearing. Because of those
handicaps, not in spite of them, Miss Helen Keller has
become a means of blessing to hosts of men and women
who find the going rough and the burden heavy. If one
could ask her the secret of radiance in the midst of
limitations, doubtless Miss Keller would reply in terms
of religion. In Boston, as a girl ten years of age, she
learned from Phillips Brooks how to let God's light and
truth shine out through a frail body. Thus she exempli-
fied the saying of Robert Browning in " Christmas
Eve ":

> " It were to be wished the flaws were fewer
> In the earthen vessel, holding treasure. . . .
> But the main thing is, does it hold good measure?
> Heaven soon sets right all other matters! "

On a vastly higher level the same principle applies to
our Lord. In the days of his flesh he fulfilled the words of
the prophet: " When we shall see him, there is no beauty
that we should desire him." For thirty-three years he let
the light of God's indwelling presence shine out through
that blessed face. In time it became more marred than
any man's. At last our Christ gave himself over to blood-
thirsty foes. They bound his hands with fetters. They
thrust on his brow a crown of thorns. They even spat
in his face. Then they nailed that dear body to an old
bloody log. When they had broken the earthen vessel

they supposed that they had extinguished the indwelling light.

To their amazement and dismay, the enemies of Christ soon discovered that his power waxed greater and greater after his death. To this very hour why does the Christian religion center at the cross? Is it not because on Calvary, and on Easter morn, as nowhere else on earth, we can behold " the light of the knowledge of the glory of God in the face of Jesus Christ "? Thus it appears that even the sinless Son of God cherished the heavenly treasure in an earthen vessel.

In view of these facts, wherein lies the secret of Christian radiance? How can you, sir, as the pastor of this congregation, become more and more like your Lord? By giving yourself into his hands, day after day, and especially by doing so now, in the spirit of prayer. To him you have long since dedicated all your gifts and your powers. For his sake you have received the most approved training for the difficult work of the ministry. Doubtless you love to sing one of our sweetest Gospel hymns:

> " Take my silver and my gold;
> Not a mite would I withhold.
> Take my intellect, and use
> Every power as Thou shalt choose."

With such sacrifices of praise and prayer the heavenly Father is well pleased, if only they are sincere. But still he expects something more in the way of dedication. To be complete, such an act of the soul ought to include your entire self. Have you ever given into God's keeping for his service all your shortcomings, your limitations, and your handicaps? If you study the life of your hero, who may be the Apostle Paul, you will find that he began to be a power in the Kingdom when he learned to look on himself as only a cracked crock. Then he put that vessel into the hands of God, to be filled with heavenly light. "The weakness that waits upon God becomes strong."

Let this, then, be your prayer: Take me, O Lord, just as I am, an earthen vessel full of flaws. Cleanse me by thy Spirit, if need be through fire. Then fill me and flood me with the light of the knowledge of the glory of God in the face of Jesus Christ. In the pulpit and in the homes of thy people use me to body forth his blessed light. Make me a means of blessing to my fellow men. So shall I give thee the glory, through Him who alone is the Light of the World. Amen.

NATIONAL HOLIDAY

I Kings 18:17–39

THE CALL OF GOD TO AMERICA

" How long halt ye between two opinions? if the Lord be God, follow him: but if Baal, then follow him." — I Kings 18:21.

TODAY we give thanks to God for our country. All over the land Christian men and women remember with gladness the ways through which he has guided us as a people. We are grateful for the strong men he has raised up to lead us in times of peril, for the freedom he has given us richly to enjoy, for the bounties of the " good earth " he has blessed, and for the privilege of sharing our mercies with his other children around the world. Throughout the homeland we give him hearty thanks because the lines have fallen unto us in pleasant places and we have a goodly heritage. Surely " he hath not dealt so with any nation."

It is proper, therefore, that we ask with the psalmist: " What fit return, Lord, can we make for all thy gifts on us bestowed? " Through his reply we may learn that God is not so much pleased with us as we are with ourselves. Thus far we have been thinking in terms of the Hebrew poets with their ascriptions of praise to the Almighty. If we are to be in accord with the will of God we must also listen to the prophets as they tell us about national shortcomings and sins. They insist that when God blesses a land he expects that country to obey his laws.

For a sobering message from the God of our nation we turn to Elijah, whom the Hebrews counted the strongest of all their prophets. In the chapter before us we find one of the most thrilling scenes in Old Testament history. Through Mendelssohn's oratorio, *Elijah,* we have learned to think of the scene on Mount Carmel as intensely dramatic. From students of classic literature we learn that serious drama involves the conflict of titanic forces. On Mount Carmel we witness a struggle unto death, to determine whether or not the Lord God of the fathers shall continue to rule over the sons and their succeeding race.

For such a contest one sees on Mount Carmel an ideal setting. As one drives northward through the heart of the Holy Land, mile after mile, one sees over on the left hand the lower end of the mountain range known as Carmel. As one looks up to that ridge of hills jutting out into the plain, one thinks of a giant plowshare ready to drive a chasm between the righteous and the wicked. On those rugged slopes one mentally re-enacts the scene where " the prophet of fire " stood singlehanded against four hundred and fifty prophets of Baal, the would-be deity of the fickle Hebrews.

When we look more closely at the record we discover that it resembles a one-act play. In the passage before us we note three successive scenes. Since they all occur at one place, with the same actors, and within a single day, we should be able to reconstruct the drama. Better still, we ought to derive from it lessons for our own land today. In the chapter as a whole we hear the Most High calling on our country for a revival of old-fashioned religion. The heart of that is loyalty to God.

Scene 1. A Crisis in the Land. An ideal drama presents someone to admire, someone to dread, and someone to follow. All this and more appeared in the contest on

Mount Carmel. In Old Testament terms the battle was soon to be joined between God and Baal. In New Testament words the decision lay between God and Mammon. In present-day speech the conflict involved God and no-God. Whatever the phrasing, there could be no compromise. The struggle must lead to "unconditional surrender."

Let us be sure that we understand the issue. In the well-known words of William James, it was living, vital, momentous. "How long halt ye between two opinions?" More literally, as the text reads in the American Revised Version: "How long go ye limping between the two sides?" Was the Hebrew nation to continue being loyal to the God of Abraham, Isaac, and Jacob? Or was it to turn aside and follow Baal, perhaps the foulest of ancient substitutes for the Living God? If the people assembled at Carmel had determined to accept Baal as their national God, the whole course of Hebrew history would have been changed. In like manner today, the Lord is calling on us in America to determine whether we shall be true to the God of our fathers or turn aside to follow some anti-God such as secularism.

In any day of spiritual crisis certain people stand out-and-out for the Living God. As the leader of such folk on Mount Carmel, the Lord raised up " the prophet of fire." With him in loyalty to the Most High God stood at least seven thousand stalwart defenders of the faith. Few of them, however, seem to have been present on Carmel. If they had been there, what could they have accomplished amid all the hosts of the Hebrew people? From that day to the present hour, in almost every land, not least in our own, the loyal followers of God have been largely outnumbered. Throughout the history of the world thus far, when has any leader such as Elijah ever been able to rally the majority of his people for an active crusade against the powers of anti-God?

On the other hand, the forces opposed to the prophet must have seemed as numberless as the sands on the seashore. As for their leader, Elijah had to contend with King Ahab, and back of him, with Queen Jezebel. Like Lady Macbeth, in Shakespeare's tragedy, Jezebel appears to have ruled over her husband and to have strengthened his hands for every evil. Both Jezebel and Ahab had sold their souls to the foes of their country and their God. With those two leaders stood four hundred and fifty prophets of Baal, and four hundred other so-called religious guides. All of them must have been imported to seduce the Hebrew people from loyalty to the faith of their fathers. When has a dramatist ever set forth a more appalling crisis?

On that fateful day of decision the masses of the people appear to have been indifferent. When the prophet of God called on them for a verdict, " the people answered him not a word." Perhaps they wondered why he should seem so excited. Doubtless they thought they could stand on the side lines and watch the contest, with no personal concern about the issue. In like manner more than a few of our people recently supposed it could make small difference to us in the Americas whether or not Hitler and Hirohito mastered the Western and the Eastern halves of our world. Few of us stopped to ask what God thought of such " benevolent neutrality."

I do not now refer to certain conscientious objectors, or to other patriotic citizens, such as the Friends, for whom I cherish high esteem. I am thinking rather of indifferent citizens like those of whom Deborah sang

after a day of crisis: " Curse ye Meroz, said the angel of
the Lord, curse ye bitterly the inhabitants thereof; because they came not to the help of the Lord, to the help
of the Lord against the mighty." When such a spirit
of passive indifference prevails in the local Church, the
living Christ voices a solemn warning: " I would that
thou wert cold or hot. So then because thou art luke-
warm, and neither cold nor hot, I will spue thee out of
my mouth."

For such a contest between titanic forces look at the
Reformation in the time of Martin Luther. When he
nailed his Ninety-five Theses on the door of the Castle
Church at Wittenberg, only a few of the people, comparatively, seem to have stood out-and-out for the God
of the Bible. On the other hand, the powers arrayed
against the Reformer were mighty. They were strongly
intrenched. They likewise stood ready for aggressive
action. But the masses of the people seem not to have
felt concerned. Thus passively they opposed the Reformation. When Martin Luther called on them to take
their stand, " the people answered him not a word." Is it
any wonder that the prophet of God often suffers from
a broken heart? What is he but " the voice of one crying
in the wilderness "? That may be why William Drum-
mond three hundred years ago sang about John the Baptist's preaching in the open country:

" There burst he forth: ' All ye whose hopes rely
    On God, with me amidst these deserts mourn;
    Repent, repent, and from old errors turn! '

" Who listened to his voice, obeyed his cry?
    Only the echoes, which he made relent,
    Rung from their flinty caves, ' Repent, Repent! ' "

Scene 2. The Contest in the Land. The contest resembled the one between David and Goliath, but on a much vaster scale, and with far more tremendous stakes. Under God, what lay in the balance was the continued survival of real religion in the land. For a parallel think of the French Revolution, which broke out in the early summer of 1789. Or else consider the Russian upheaval, which took place in the late summer of 1917. In each case the National Church had grown so corrupt and useless that the new leaders of the land strove to banish the God of their fathers. In succeeding years other leaders have been obliged to let him come back through some side door. From the aftereffects of those experiments with no-God, both France and Russia still suffer today.

In the contest between Elijah and the prophets of Baal the spokesman for God displayed rare sportsmanship. Though outnumbered by a host of alien contenders, he offered them the first opportunity to call down fire from the heavens. If Baal was a sun-god, as some scholars believe, Elijah gave his foes every advantage when he proposed a contest involving fire from above. Evidently he wished to convince the wavering people that Baal was no-God, and that those who succumbed to the blandishments of his henchmen were turning against the Almighty. Well did the prophet know that he was opposing the deadliest treason.

The progress of the contest ought to rivet the attention of everyone here today. If the issue did not involve the life and the honor of the nation, the record might seem almost farcical. Surely it presents ridicule and irony, satire and sarcasm, unexcelled even by Juvenal or Dean Swift. Hour after hour, with growing frenzy, like the wildest dervishes from the desert, the devotees of anti-God scream and cut themselves until the blood gushes out. Still there comes no response from the sullen skies. Evidently anti-God must be no-God! As if to increase the fury of those frantic endeavors to bring down fire from the sky, the prophet of Jehovah exclaims: " Cry aloud: for he is a god; either he is talking, or he is pursuing, or he is in a journey, or peradventure he sleepeth, and must be awaked." But still there appears no sign of fire from the skies.

The spirit of Elijah makes one think of John Knox. When such a crusader for God faces a woman like Mary Queen of Scots, there must be iron in the man's blood and fire in his words. Thus it proved four hundred years ago when Knox cried out to God, " Give me Scotland or I die! " In answer to his prayer the Lord used him in bringing the people a large measure of righteousness and power. From that day forward, at least until the present generation, the history of Scotland continued to be that of repeated revivals. One crusader after another, with courage and tenacity like that of John Knox, summoned the people to the service of the Most High: " If the Lord be God, follow him! " What a contest in the nation!

Scene 3. The Conquest of the Land. From the contest Elijah emerges the victor. But he ascribes all the glory to God. In the eyes of succeeding ages, this man seemed the mightiest of all the Hebrew prophets, who were the most powerful men of the Hebrew race. Like those other moral and spiritual giants, this man knew that all his power and his conquest had come from the Living God.

Such a working philosophy of religion does not suffer

a leader to remain idle. Because he trusted in God for victory, Elijah became a man of heroic action. So did Martin Luther, and John Knox. Each of them toiled as though everything depended on him alone. For the Lord his God, Elijah performed on Mount Carmel every service that mortal man could render. There he led in erecting an altar, and he must have built it well. By faith he had learned that whatever we mortals do for God ought to be performed with the utmost skill and care. Only our best can be worthy of our King. From that altar on Mount Carmel we should learn in passing: God expects us to do for him all that lies within the powers he has bestowed.

When the altar was ready, Elijah called on the Lord to do for men what they could not do for him; that is, send down the fire. Because the Lord heard that plea and sent that flame, to consume the waiting sacrifice, Elijah became known as "the prophet of fire." If he could have had his way, he would have preferred to be called a man of prayer. According to the Apostle James, "Elias was a man subject to like passions as we are." Unlike many of us, he knew how to pray in a crisis. Concerning his victory at Mount Carmel, the apostle wrote: "The effectual fervent prayer of a righteous man availeth much." In *The Complete Bible: An American Translation,* by Drs. Smith and Goodspeed, the verse reads: "An upright man can do a great deal by prayer when he tries."

On Mount Carmel the fire of God fell and consumed the waiting sacrifice. At Pentecost the fire came down and entered into the hearts of the praying disciples. In England two hundred years ago the fire descended largely because of the faith and the prayers of John Wesley. In many ways he differed from Elijah, as well as from Martin Luther, or John Knox. But the spirit of Wesley also kept burning with loyalty to God. Apart from the Wesleyan Movement, so Lecky and other secular historians tell us, England would have experienced some such social cataclysm as the French Revolution.

The response of the people at Mount Carmel deserves more than a passing glance. When the prophet first spoke to them on behalf of God, " the people answered him not a word." But when Jehovah manifested his power by sending the fire, those same people fell on their faces and cried out: " The Lord he is the God! the Lord, he is the God! " Would that it might be so today! Perhaps that might be the case in every community if there were a leader such as Elijah. He would bring God's people face to face with their spiritual foes, and then lead in prayer for fire from heaven.

" The saddest fact about our generation is that we never have witnessed a revival of religion." So speaks one of the wisest leaders in the Scottish Church today. Despite repeated warnings from God in times of peace and in days of war, we in the States also have not fallen down on our faces and cried out to God for mercy. At times some of us assemble in our Churches to give thanks for Martin Luther, John Knox, and John Wesley. But should we not also humble ourselves before the God whom each of them served, and then beseech his blessing upon our sinful nation?

" All of this may be true," someone here replies, " but what has it to do with me? " At the very least, my friend, you can be out-and-out for God. When some Elijah appears, you can rally to his call. You can take your stand with the seven thousand who will never bow the knee to any substitute for the Living God. But why wait for the appearing of Elijah and his seven thousand? John Wesley used to say that if he had three hundred men who loved no one but God, hated naught but sin, and followed no one but the Saviour, with such a band he could win his world for Christ and the Church.

Be out-and-out for God! Then you will pray. Implore God now to send a revival. Ask that it may begin here in our Church. Thus you may witness at home a drama as moving as that one of old on Mount Carmel.

" How long halt ye between two opinions? if the Lord be God, follow him: but if Baal, then follow him." In response to this ringing appeal let every heart cry out: " The Lord, he is the God; the Lord, he is the God."

VACATION TIME

Ps. 121; Matt. 11:28–30

THE PSALM FOR MIDSUMMER

" The Lord shall preserve thy going out and thy coming in from this time forth, and even for evermore." — Ps. 121:8.

AT THIS time of the year everyone longs to take the wings of the morning and fly away to the hills. At such a season one ought to sing or read the Traveler's Psalm. At the breakfast table in a certain home, if a son or daughter is about to depart for a journey, or if a loved one has come from afar, the members of the household join in repeating the One Hundred and Twenty-first Psalm. Then they unite in a brief prayer, which has to do with traveling mercies. Especially should our song be dear to the Christian railroad man. To him life means an endless succession of goings out and comings in.

At this vacation season no part of the Bible could be more fitting. The Traveler's Psalm appears to have been sung by the Children of Israel as they journeyed up to Jerusalem to enjoy one of the annual feasts. Those festal seasons ordained of God served as the red-letter days of the Hebrew year. Then, if ever on earth, joy was unconfined. Leaving their homes and their daily toil, with all its dull, drab drudgery, those farmers and their households would sing as they wended their way up to the City of God: " I will lift up mine eyes unto the hills, from whence cometh my help." That help came from the hills because there the Hebrews found the Living God.

In this little lyric of joy, the dominant note rings out

six times: " He that keepeth thee "; " He that keepeth Israel "; " The Lord is thy keeper "; " The Lord shall preserve thee "; " He shall preserve thy soul "; " The Lord shall preserve thy going out and thy coming in from this time forth, and even for evermore." In the Hebrew the words " keep " and " preserve " are exactly the same.

The truth that undergirds the psalm is the keeping power of God, otherwise known as Providence. Literally this word from the Latin means that God is the Supreme Provider. Carefully he foresees the needs of his children. Tenderly he cares for them all, as though he had only one. In the Traveler's Psalm these truths appear in the form of word pictures. Let us look at them now, from four points of view.

1. *The God of the Waiting Hills.* " I will lift up mine eyes unto the hills, from whence cometh my help." To the Hebrews the hills stood as silent witnesses of God's power. Thus the beckoning hills encouraged the man of faith to look up, not down; to look without, not within; to look forward, not backward. Up in those beckoning hills the pilgrim could catch a glimpse of far horizons. He could likewise hope to enjoy an air of increased visibility. In other words, he could feel that heaven was near, and that life on earth was good. Much the same spirit breathes out from the song by Henry van Dyke:

" O who will walk a mile with me
    Along life's weary way?
A friend whose heart has eyes to see
The stars shine out o'er the darkening lea,
And the quiet rest at the end o' the day, —
A friend who knows, and dares to say,
The brave, sweet words that cheer the way
    Where he walks a mile with me.

" With such a comrade, such a friend,
I fain would walk till journey's end,
Through summer sunshine, winter rain,
And then? — Farewell, we shall meet again! "

All this and more one ought to mean by the open-air treatment of the soul. When it becomes weary and forlorn, what does it need so much as a journey into the beckoning hills? In our part of the world why should the summer season be largely free from disease? Is it not because we now enjoy abundance of sunshine and fresh air in God's boundless outdoors? " If the secret of the new surgery is cleanness, that of the new medicine is fresh air." But why speak of such a soothing balm as new? Did not the Lord's people of old live much in the open air? Fortunately one need not journey afar in order to enjoy the breezes that blow from the mountains of God. Even while one tarries at home and keeps on at work, or else lies on a bed of weakness and pain, one can lift up the eyes of the soul and look unto the hills that may appear only in memory and in hope.

The vital fact just now is that in those hills, whether or not they are seen, one is able to find the Living God. This truth shines out from almost every page of *The Pilgrim's Progress*. Even while John Bunyan was an inmate of Bedford Jail, in his heart he could journey far away over the hills of the land that he loved. After a while his pilgrimage led him to the Hill Difficulty. There he found lodging in the House Beautiful. Erelong he fell asleep in " a large upper chamber, whose windows opened towards the sun-rising." The name of this resting place was Peace. In the visions of the night he beheld the Delectable Mountains. When he asked about the name of the country he learned that it was Im-

manuel's Land. From there he found that he could behold the gates of the Celestial City.

2. *The God of the Sleepless Watch.* To us who dwell
in mortal bodies the thought of a midsummer trip leads
us on to the prospect of rest in sleep. To the one who is
weary and sick at heart, sleep comes as a boon from
heaven above. But for the Father of us all there can be
no folding of the hands in slumber. Rather is he The
God of the Sleepless Watch. Why does the mother hang
over the cradle at midnight when her little lad seems to
be burning up with fever? Is it not because of her love?
That must be why the prophet says: " As one whom his
mother comforteth, so will I comfort you." Because He
never slumbers or sleeps, he can watch over every child
of his heart, especially the one who most needs tender
care.

In much the same manner the Lord God watches over
his Church. That is what we understand by the psalmist's words, " He that keepeth Israel." Looking back over
all the ages since the unknown bard sang about The God
of the Sleepless Watch, we can bear witness that he has
never failed to look after his Church. In the midst of
accident and danger, in times of persecution and distress, he has kept the Church of our Redeemer alive and
strong. Better still, the Lord God has pledged his honor
that while the bush may burn, it shall never be consumed.

If the waiting hills tell of his almighty power, the
sleepless watch betokens his perseverance. He that has
begun a blessed work in the Church of Christ shall never
cease until its mission on earth is complete. Whenever
we ascribe praises to our God, we ought to give thanks

for his perseverance. " Hast thou not known? hast thou not heard, that the everlasting God, . . . the Creator of the ends of the earth, fainteth not, neither is weary? . . . He giveth power to the faint; and to them that have no might he increaseth strength." Such is the saint's assurance concerning The God of the Sleepless Watch.

3. *The God of the Friendly Shade*. Especially when the heat becomes intense, the shade serves as a symbol of protection. Thus The God of the Waiting Hills and of the Sleepless Watch likewise offers rest for weary souls. That must be why the prophet tells about " the shadow of a great rock in a weary land." Much the same blessing appears in the words of the Master: " Come unto me, all ye that labour and are heavy laden, and I will give you rest. Take my yoke upon you, and learn of me; for I am meek and lowly in heart: and ye shall find rest unto your souls."

In the midst of summer there may be special need of God's protection. Whenever one journeys through a land of hills and valleys, whether by day or night, one cannot know what lies round the next bend in the road, but still there need be no hesitation or fear. Living day by day is like traveling over a sky-line trail that leads hither and thither among the mountains. Nevertheless, remember that " the Lord is thy keeper." Even amid the densest fog or the deepest snow, the child of God can rest in the assurance, " He knoweth the way that I take." When we thank God for all his goodness, therefore, let us be sure to include his loving protection.

In 403 A.D., Chrysostom suffered banishment from Constantinople, where he had served as the archbishop. Knowing that the charges against him were unjust, he wrote to a friend: " When I was driven from the city I felt no anxiety but said to myself, ' If the Empress wishes to banish me, let her do so; the earth is the Lord's. If she wants to have me sawn asunder, I have Isaiah for an example. If she wants me to be drowned, I think of Jonah. If I am to be thrown into the fire, the three men in the furnace suffered the same. If I am to be cast before wild beasts, I remember Daniel in the lions' den. If she wants me to be stoned, I have before me Stephen, the first martyr.' " " The Lord is thy keeper! "

The last part of the midsummer psalm is the best of all.

4. *The God of the Winding Road.* If those other pictures tell of God's power, his perseverance, and his protection, these closing verses sing about his peace. " The Lord shall preserve thy going out and thy coming in from this time forth, and even for evermore." In the midst of busy life today, with all its uncertainties and perils, as well as its alarms and fears, what does the average man need so much as the calm assurance that God is leading him safely home?

> " Peace, perfect peace, our future all unknown?
> Jesus we know, and He is on the throne."

According to a wise old saying, the best part of any journey is the joy of coming home. In like manner, The God of the Winding Road bids us think of life here below as traveling toward the heavenly home. That must have been the spirit in which David Livingstone bade farewell to his loved ones when he was about to sail away to darkest Africa. On the morning of November 17, 1840, he read with his loved ones this Traveler's Psalm.

Then they knelt to pray that The God of the Winding Road would keep the son who was traveling afar, as well as those who tarried at home, because of the Father's will.

In the heart of David Livingstone, while wandering through the jungles and the swamps of Africa, there was ever the thought of home. That was where someday he hoped to enjoy the fellowship of his father and mother. Alas, the missionary was never again to look upon the face of his father in the flesh! Still the son could keep on singing the Traveler's Psalm. By faith the missionary knew that The God of the Winding Road would lead his missionary servant at last to the heavenly home. Hence, the Scottish pioneer could have entered into the spirit of the lines from Joyce Kilmer:

" And the only reason a road is good, as every wanderer
      knows,
   Is just because of the homes, the homes, the homes to which
      it goes! . . .

" It's a rough road and a steep road and it stretches broad
      and far,
   But it leads at last to a Golden Town where Golden Houses
      are."

As a lover of the psalms, however, Livingstone would have responded much more quickly to the song of the shepherd. Nowhere on earth do the children of God love the Twenty-third Psalm more dearly than in Scotland. When they come to the closing stanza of the metrical version their eyes may fill with tears. They are thinking in terms of arriving safely at the Father's home. Doubtless they know that they are reading something into the words of the shepherd poet. But, since they are Christians, why should they not interpret The Book of Psalms in the fuller light that streams from the face of our risen Lord and Saviour?

> " Goodness and mercy all my life
> Shall surely follow me;
> And in God's House forevermore
> My dwelling place shall be."

Thus we have thought together about the four ascending stages in the psalm for midsummer. At heart this sort of religion must be intensely personal. From beginning to end the Traveler's Psalm keeps singing about the loving care of God for his children one by one.

Now he wishes each of you to make this psalm your own. In order to do so, commit the words to memory. That will be much easier if you recall the four picture phrases suggested by the poem: The God of the Waiting Hills; The God of the Sleepless Watch; The God of the Friendly Shade; and The God of the Winding Road. All four of them sing about the Living God. They tell of his Power and his Perseverance, his Protection and his Peace, both now and forevermore.

Is the God of the psalmist your personal God? If so, you can fare forth on life's journey unafraid. Begin now to form the habit of lifting up your eyes to the hills. There you will behold the God of the midsummer psalm. He in turn will keep your going out and your coming in, from this time forth and even forevermore.

LABOR SUNDAY
Micah 4:1–5; Rev. 6:1–11

THE WILL OF GOD FOR A WORKINGMAN
" They shall sit every man under his vine and under his fig tree; and none shall make them afraid." — Micah 4:4.

THE picture of the vine and the fig tree comes from an artist in the use of words. Because his heart is moved, the seer writes with beauty. Hence, the text appeals to the eye of the soul. The prophet wishes each of us to see the will of God for a workingman. The time in view is after the world has been at war. Thus the earlier part of the vision has to do with the advent of peace. The latter portion, which concerns us now, shows the fruits of peace for a workingman. The one before us serves God as a tiller of the ground. But the same principles apply to everyone who does the will of the Almighty with a loyal heart and two brown hands.

The welfare of the workingman must ever be dear to the heart of God. When our Lord came from heaven to redeem our world from sin, he toiled for a while as a carpenter in Nazareth. A few years later, when his critics protested against his way of using God-given powers, the " Master Workman of the race " uttered a truth doubly precious on Labor Sunday: " My Father worketh hitherto, and I work." Thus our Lord took his place in the forefront of the Hebrew seers, all of whom demanded justice for earth's toilers. Especially did Micah speak out boldly as the prophet of the working people.

The Old Testament and the New alike have a message for the laboring man. Hence, the Church today should

not hold its peace. What better can we do on Labor
Sunday than try to translate the glowing imagery of
Micah into practical terms of today? What, then, does
the prophet teach when he bids us see the man of toil
sitting under his vine and fig tree? The picture must
concern that promised age of gold when the sons of earth
shall learn war no more. Then the workingman, like
everyone else, will enjoy the " four freedoms " that now
have become famous. Instead of serving as a political
slogan, however, the four freedoms should become the
right of every man who does his share of the world's
work.

Of the four freedoms, every citizen in our land enjoys
the first and the second, at least in a large degree. Except
for restraints imposed during days of war, the laboring
man in the States need be little concerned about securing freedom of speech and liberty to worship. Rather
should he use these rights with care lest he lose them
through neglect. Meanwhile, we should never be content until these gifts of God are the possession of every
man on whom the sun keeps shining. When we consider
the third freedom and the fourth, however, we must
confess that we have failed. Here in the homeland we
have far to go before we can assure every honest workingman freedom from want and freedom from fear.
These are the two gifts of God promised in our text.

The workingman seated at ease under his vine and
fig tree affords:

1. *A Symbol of Freedom from Want.* In the days of
rebuilding after every war the most crucial problem
seems to be that of unemployment. When " hushed is
the cannon's roar, and the only sound from its rusty

throat is a wren's or a bluebird's note," the question must arise: Is the workingman to remain free from want, or is he to suffer again from having nothing to do?

Over in England wise men have begun to face this question squarely. In November, 1942, acting under orders from the Crown, Sir William Beveridge presented his voluminous report. It is full of practical suggestions about doing away with want in times of peace. Obviously, few of us are qualified to appraise the Beveridge Plan, or any of its successors. Nothing should prevent us, however, from seeing that it marked an epoch in the history of the modern world. In the very midst of earth's most devastating war the leaders of the British Empire started a heroic endeavor to carry out the ideals of the Hebrew prophet.

What Micah foretold in words of rhythmical beauty, the British economist expresses in workaday prose: " The aim of the Plan is to abolish want by insuring that every citizen willing to serve according to his powers has at all times an income sufficient to meet his responsible duties." Once again Sir William assures us: " The Plan is not one of giving to everybody something for nothing, and without trouble, or something that will free the recipients thereafter from personal responsibilities." Thus the social reformer agrees with the prophet of old that there must be no encouragement of luxury, and no incentive for idleness. On the other hand, everyone who toils aright should receive the due reward of his labors. The man who works should not suffer want. Neither should his wife and children.

If there is to be freedom from want, there must be no lack of work for willing hands. According to the Beveridge Report, both in Britain and in America there have

been two periods of recent history when the laboring
people have been reasonably free from want arising
through lack of work. The first era of the sort came during World War I, and the second during World War
II. In the text from Micah the seer boldly proclaims that
God wishes his children to be free from want when there
is no war. The question may arise: How can we insure
work for waiting hands during times of peace? Let this
be the answer: The God who loves the laboring man is
ready to guide those who wish to do his will.

The picture of the workingman under his vine and fig
tree makes one think of a farmer seated in his grove of
fruit trees, or a city toiler with a plot of ground large
enough to allow room for a garden. Whatever the setting,
the picture shows a workingman able to support his
loved ones as human beings made in the image of God.
According to an American statesman, Vice-President
Henry A. Wallace, who believes in the honest toiler,
" There is enough wheat to feed the world; there is
enough stone and brick and lumber to house the world;
there is enough cotton and wool to clothe the whole
human family." In other words, says this Christian
statesman, the God of heaven provides for all the physical needs of his children. But, alas, we as stewards of his
bounty have not learned how to make good use of what
he has given. In places of leadership we need men like
Joseph and Herbert Hoover.

The laboring man sitting at rest in his garden also
symbolizes what we know as solid comfort. Not only is
there work for willing hands; there is also rest for the
weary body. In his well-known painting, *The Angelus,*
Jean F. Millet interprets the life of rural France. It consists of work, love, and worship. The picture doubtless

presents the facts about those peasants, but the Hebrew prophet causes one to dream of something better. Why should that French wife and mother have to toil out in the fields? Since the sun is about to set, why should not the husband and father also be sitting at home, enjoying his rest after a day of arduous toil?

The late Dr. Richard C. Cabot, of the Harvard Medical School, brings us closer to the will of God. In his book of practical wisdom, *What Men Live By,* this expert in social medicine insists that the basic human needs are work, play, love, and worship. Note the emphasis on recreation. If a man of middle age has been toiling out in the sun, or stoking a furnace in a factory, he may not feel the need of play. But he deserves time and opportunity for rest and relaxation, amid scenes of beauty and peace.

Such desires ought to center at home. Especially as a man grows older, he should think of work and rest, love and worship, together with his dear ones in the family circle. To sit out under the trees in one's own garden, there to watch the children or children's children at play — what could seem more like heaven on earth? Is the Lord God asking too much of a nation when he bids it provide for the comfort of every household where the husband and father manfully toils day after day and year after year?

That is the ideal. What are the facts? A current play, *Hope for a Harvest,* by Sophie Treadwell, deals with " a country slum." In the Far West an Italian succeeds where his neighbors fail. Without boasting he can say: " We live, my wife and I, and so do our little ones. We live well. Farming is not just a business of selling crops. Farming is the way to live." In reply a young woman from the " country slum " near by says to him, wistfully: " That's just what I want to find here. A life! " A little later she adds, " Everybody stakes his life on something or other."

In recent years numerous playwrights and novelists have called our attention to the plight of migrant farmers, sharecroppers, tenement dwellers, and other millions who never can hope to rest under vines and fig trees of their own planting. Some of those folk cannot even raise cabbage and onions! They must move too often. The stark realism of *Tobacco Road* and *The Grapes of Wrath* makes some of us shudder. Needless to say, such writers go too far in exploiting the filthiest aspects of sex. As the Apostle Paul tells us, " It is a shame even to speak of those things." However, he himself felt forced to discuss them more than once, and that with utmost frankness. In almost every epistle he makes one ashamed that there is still so much filth to exploit.

If Paul were living now, he would agree with Albert Schweitzer: " The only standard by which we can measure a civilization is by the value it places on human life." This contemporary thinker defines civilization as " the progress of individuals and nations so that the struggle for existence becomes less intense." From his point of view, which is clearly Biblical, has our country even begun to be civilized? Not if we are to believe what a Negro girl says about sharecroppers. Her name is Carmen Williams. Her testimony appears in *The Crisis,* an American " Record of the Darker Races ":

" But for the grace of God I too should be one of them. I should be denied proper food, adequate shelter, and the chance to attend school long enough to acquire a usable education. . . . After all, it seems so little to ask in a land of plenty: food, knowledge, and shelter to make people truly fit to serve the land they know as home, and against which they have never plotted treason." If the statement sounds extreme, remember that similar conditions among God's suffering poor once led to the French Revolution, and more recently to the Russian upheaval. God forbid that we in the United States should ever witness such an upsurging of subterranean forces let loose for hellish destruction. Let us, therefore, resolve that by God's grace we shall set our toiling millions free from want.

2. *A Symbol of Freedom from Fear.* After these glowing words about rest in the garden, the prophet continues: "And none shall make them afraid." The specific teaching here relates to war and peace. How can there be security for the workingman, or anyone else, in a world that must shiver while preparing for war after war? Let us look at the subject from another point of view. Apart from war, what has the laboring man to fear? Though he may feel secure about holding his job, and getting his envelope, this next week, what of the unknown future?

Some of the fears that beset a thoughtful toiler have to do with sickness and accident. A few years ago the commissioner of health in a Southern city, not among the mountains, reported that the county where he lived included more than a hundred practicing physicians. Despite the fact that the surrounding rural districts contained more people than the central city, all but three of the doctors made that their home. The state official declared that in the entire county he did not know a single farmer who could afford to carry his family through an

epidemic of typhoid fever. If you were one of those farmers, would you not feel concerned about the care of
your loved ones in case of prolonged illness? Is there no
call for some kind of " social medicine " in our rural
districts?

Other fears have to do with old age. How long will the
city toiler be able to command the strength and the
energy, the quickness of eye and the alertness of hand,
that he must possess in order to master a vast machine?
Someday he will be thrown on the scrap heap. Then who
will care for his wife and children? Well does he know
that a scrap pile becomes the most forbidding spot in
town or countryside. Why should he not shudder when
he fears that he may soon be cast aside as a piece of humanity's wastage?

You will note that all these fears concern a man's
loved ones. The person in view works hard and saves
his money. He does not drink or gamble. Nevertheless,
under peacetime conditions, he must wonder what will
become of his dear ones when he is cast aside. Never can
he or they willingly accept charity, whether it comes
from the Government or from the Church. Never would
such sturdy citizens dream of stooping to accept a
" dole." Rather do they pray for the coming of a golden
era when the toiler can safeguard the future of all those
who bear his name.

These fears may be intensified by war and its aftermath. Some of us boys used thoughtlessly to sing about
" marching through Georgia." More recently as adults
we have often heard about " the scorched earth." But
do we remember that all four foul horsemen of the
Apocalypse follow swiftly in the wake of " total war "?
Do we forget that those who suffer most must be the

country toilers, with their wives and children? Equally pitiful must be the plight of able-bodied men turned rudely away from the barred gates of city mills where they have been welcome in days of war. How can those toiling millions ever hope to be free from fear?

> " Lord God of Hosts, be with us yet,
> Lest we forget — lest we forget! "

Thus we have thought about God's ideal for the workingman. At the basis of all these aspirations lies old-fashioned Biblical justice. Needless to say, the forces of labor have not always lived up to their side of working contracts. For instance, their leaders have never been able to justify the typical " sit-down strike." Many of us are not willing to help to provide soft cushions for sit-down strikers! But we are intent upon securing justice for every man who honorably toils. We are even more concerned about untold hosts of human beings, both black and white, who have neither the skill nor the chance to join any branch of organized labor. To whom shall the submerged tenth look for freedom from want and from fear? Should they not turn to God and his Church? At least we can assure them of our sympathy and prayers. But really we ought to do more, vastly more.

Many of us have never suffered from such want and fear. In Rachel Field's last novel, *And Now Tomorrow*, she put into the mouth of a certain character these moving words: " You've always had this thing they call security. You've never known what it was to wonder where your next meal was coming from, or a new pair of shoes, or a place to sleep at night." Such experiences our Saviour knew. So, in a different fashion, did Abraham Lincoln. In his Second Inaugural Address he spoke out of a heart that had tasted the bitterness of want and fear.

He had in view the victims of war, but the same ideals
of Christian helpfulness should reach out and embrace
all who through no fault of their own must suffer as the
victims of want and fear:

" With malice toward none; with charity for all; with
firmness in the right, as God gives us to see the right, let
us strive on to finish the work we are in, to bind up the
nation's wounds, to care for him who shall have borne
the battle, and for his widow and orphans, to do all
which may achieve a just and lasting peace among ourselves and all mankind." Such a vision has come more
recently from Edwin Markham in his *Poems of Justice:*

> " We are all blind until we see
>   That in the human plan
> Nothing is worth the making if
>   It does not make the man.
>
> " Why build these cities glorious
>   If man unbuilded goes?
> In vain we build the work, unless
>   The builder also grows."

Long ere this stage of the discussion someone may be
asking, " What have all these things to do with our religion? " The question is fair; let the reply be frank. We
derive our Christianity mainly from the Bible, notably
from the New Testament. In the Scriptures we find the
ethical ideals of the prophets, and of our Lord, as well
as of his apostles. If I understand the Holy Scriptures
aright, they command the Church to take no rest until
our " good earth " has become a fit dwelling place for the
sons and daughters of the workingman. From this practical point of view, why not search the Scriptures and learn
what they reveal about the will of God for the friend who
toils with his hands? Remember that he labors for us, as
well as for God.

Over in Britain Lloyd George once was asked what the Church should do in helping the nation to get rid of poverty. Here follows a portion of his reply: " The Church is not to urge or advocate any specific measure of social reform. . . . The Church must rouse the national conscience to the existence of these evils and to the Nation's responsibility for dealing with them. The Church ought to be like a limelight turned on the slum lands, to shame those in authority into doing something. It is not for the Church to draft Housing Acts, or to enter into political propaganda, or to support any particular measure. But let her hunt out evil conditions, expose them, drag them into the light of day. When they come to be dealt with, let her . . . hand them over to the secular arm." After such words of practical wisdom, would that all the redeemed of the Lord might say: " Amen! Let us arise and help to build that sort of world! "

Ere we go from the " house of prayer for all people," let us bow down and face this matter squarely. Let us begin by thanking God for those whose toil enables us to enjoy home and Church, with all the other good things of earth. Then let us resolve, one by one, to do our full share in setting every true laboring man free from want and free from fear. Is not the workingman our brother? Is he not made in the image of God? Is he not walking in the footsteps of Christ the Carpenter? Then let each of us determine to pray and work for the coming of the day when the vision of the prophet shall become a fact of everyday life:

> " They shall sit every man under his vine and his
> fig tree; and none shall make them afraid."

PUBLIC SCHOOL DAY

Prov. 8:1–17; I Cor. 13

THE GOLDEN TEXT OF A TEACHER

*" They that be teachers shall shine as the brightness of the firmament, and they that turn many to righteousness as the stars for ever and ever." —
Dan. 12:3 (Hebrew) .*

TODAY we should thank God for the teachers in our public schools. Tomorrow we shall send our boys and girls, with our youths and maidens, to the schoolrooms. There they will learn the truths that will make them free and strong. Well do we know that the future of our world, under God, rests largely in the hands of our children and our children's children. Hence we should feel much concerned about the teachers to whom we in the States commit the keeping of twenty-five million boys and girls. Fortunately, with few exceptions, the teachers in our public schools appear to be worthy of their high calling.

What, then, is the God-given mission of the public-school teacher? How does this calling differ from other ways of being useful? Above all, what are the rewards, both on earth and in heaven? For light on such questions we turn to the Bible. In The Book of Daniel the verses surrounding our text are difficult. They have to do with " the tragic sense of life," in a day of calamity and chaos. For that very reason the words of the ancient seer ought to meet with a welcome in a day when the world has been at war, and when almost every land needs to lay new foundations deep and strong.

The text in the Hebrew assures the blessing of God for teachers who turn many to righteousness. Amid all the uncertainty that surrounds the text, one truth shines out clearly: The blessing of God abides upon every teacher who is faithful to this God-given mission. Hence our text may serve as a guiding star for the one whom the Lord calls to serve as a teacher. In His eyes there could be no more signal token of honor.

1. *The God-given Work of the Teacher.* Such a mission is close to that of the minister. He too should turn many to righteousness. Every public-school " teacher come from God " ought to feel concerned for the boys and girls, one by one. According to Pestalozzi, the patron saint of many a modern school, " The essential principle of education is not teaching; it is love." Whatever the subject in hand, the aim should be to guide young feet into paths of righteousness and honor. Sooner or later, the earlier the better, every boy should discover himself and his God-given powers. In this high privilege of helping him to find the meaning and the glory of his body and his soul, the teacher at school and the mother at home should work together as handmaidens of the Lord.

The teacher should also guide the pupil in learning how to live. The latter should both " live to learn, and learn to live." When once he has formed the habit of working hard, thinking straight, and living aright, he has begun to master the finest of all the fine arts. That is the art of getting along with people, and not trying to exist like Robinson Crusoe on his lonely isle. All unconsciously, day after day, while solving the problems in hand, the pupil should be entering into the secrets of the life that is planned according to the will of God.

Ideally, every growing boy or girl should get right with God. In the oft-quoted words of Horace Bush-

nell, " The child is to grow up as a Christian, and never
know himself as being otherwise." According to Pestalozzi, " The child accustomed to pray, to think, and to
work, is already more than half educated." On the other
hand, if he is not so trained, he is scarcely educated at all.

How to attain such ideals in a democracy we in the
States have yet to discover. Meanwhile, in many of our
public schools we are rearing a generation of pagans.
Why, then, should we not insist that every teacher begin
turning the hearts of the pupils towards truth and
righteousness? Fortunately, religion can be caught more
quickly than it can be taught. Without promoting any
sort of sectarianism, or interfering with the religious
training of any home or Church, the Christian teacher
can quietly pray for her pupils, one by one. Little by
little, she can induce them to follow in her Master's
footsteps. " Allured to brighter worlds," she can lead
the way.

Every teacher knows that the planned life must have
a foundation. In any career that is to be strong and useful
the basic fact must be righteousness. That means being
right with God, right with others, right with self. Surely
that is what our war-swept world needs today. What
would we not give for a rising generation of young folk
reared to promote righteousness and peace? In Germany,
as in many another land, if the teachers and the parents
now start turning the footsteps of growing boys into
paths of honor and peace, in years to come there will be
hope for a warless world. " They that be teachers
shall . . . turn many to righteousness."

2. *Our Current Neglect of the Teacher.* Thus far we
have been looking at lofty ideals. Now let us face ugly

facts. One of them concerns the teacher's prestige. In our public schools, in our colleges, and in schools of higher learning, the rewards and the éclat go to the executives, and not to the teachers. The Hall of Fame at New York University now enrolls the names of seventy-three American men and women whom the world delights to honor. Among them all only two, Louis Agassiz and Asa Gray, have been chosen mainly because of their work as teachers.

Among the other seventy-one heroes enrolled in the Hall of Fame, one of the most worthy was James Russell Lowell. Doubtless he was selected because of his public services, as well as his literary work. But his life seems to have been spent largely as a teacher. On his seventieth birthday, a host of his admirers assembled at a banquet in his honor. The exercises included glowing tributes to his achievements as a public servant and as a writer. But there was no allusion to his work as a teacher. Later one of his most illustrious pupils, Professor Barrett Wendell, called Lowell's attention to the omission, and then spoke of him as the most inspiring teacher in all that generation. The old gentleman's face lighted up as he replied: " I am glad you said that! I had been wondering if I had not wasted half my life! "

Many a public-school teacher now at work is tempted to wonder if she has not wasted practically all her God-given powers. From quarters high and low she keeps hearing about freedom of speech and freedom of worship, freedom from want and freedom from fear. In her darker hours she asks herself whether or not she enjoys any one of the four. If ever she thinks of her declining days in terms of money, she knows that she receives less by the year than the untutored fellow who drives the milk wagon or the one who serves on a laundry route. In short, " we treat no other friend so ill " as the public-school teacher.

Worst of all, in its way, is our lack of gratitude. Who among us when young ever thanked his teacher at the end of the year? How many of us even paused to say good-by? How many letters of appreciation or invitations to dinner do we now send to these guardian angels of our children? In cases not a few, none at all! The reason often is sheer thoughtlessness, which is only another name for sin.

One of our popular radio preachers, Dr. William L. Stidger, reports that a few years ago just before Thanksgiving he sat with a group of friends who were discussing how to be grateful when times are hard. In his turn he told of his thankfulness for a certain high-school teacher. A generation ago she had introduced him to Tennyson's poems. Thus she had awakened in the lad a lifelong concern for literature.

A member of the group asked Dr. Stidger if he had ever thanked his teacher of bygone years. He acknowledged that he had not, but he vowed that he would write her a letter at once. From place to place that missive was forwarded until at last it reached her in a distant town. Her reply came back in a feeble scrawl, which made the strong man weep:

" I cannot tell you how much your note has meant to me. I am now in my eighties, living alone in a small room, cooking my own meals, lowly, and like the last leaf of fall lingering behind.

" You will be interested to know that I taught school

for fifty years, and that yours is the first note of appreciation I ever received. It came on a blue, cold morning, and cheered me as nothing has done in years."

3. *The Abiding Influence of the Teacher.* According to the words of the prophet, the " teacher come from God" shall shine as one of the stars, for ever and ever. Doubtless these glowing words point to the life beyond. Even so, we ought to consider the abiding influence of the public-school teacher while still on earth. All unconsciously, calling no attention to herself, she lets her light shine into the hearts and homes of boys and girls, many of whom will never know how much they are indebted to her quiet charm.

According to Sir James M. Barrie, if a gentlewoman has charm, she needs little else; if she has not, nothing else can take its place. For instance, who can account for the magic spell that Alice Freeman Palmer cast over the students at Wellesley College, and over the servant girls in the slums of Boston? Surely the secret lay in the charm of her personality. That was her gift from God, to be used for his glory.

The influence of such a teacher abides through the years. It is the outpouring of love that endures through time and eternity. Long after she has fallen asleep, perhaps in loneliness and penury, the seeds that she has sown in hearts and lives will keep on producing a harvest of truth and joy. If it were possible to compile a list of the men and the women who have done most to push our old world out into the sunlight, the largest groups of all would be the parents and the teachers.

As living examples of earth's teachers, think of Moses, Samuel, and Ezra; of John, James, and Paul; of Pestalozzi, Froebel, and Robert Raikes; of Horace Mann, Mark Hopkins, and Mary Lyon; as well as a host that no one can number. Their names are all written large in God's book of remembrance.

God never forgets his chosen teachers. " When Earth's last picture is painted," and the world's last lesson is learned, " the Master of All Good Workmen " will reward these friends who have helped him to mold human hearts and lives. " They that be teachers shall shine as . . . the stars " in the sky. While hard at work here below, and often poorly recompensed, they have been laying up the richest of eternal treasures.

The way to become rich in the treasures of the heart, as Alice Freeman Palmer used to remind other teachers, is to invest time and strength in human beings, especially boys and girls. The men and women who strive after things to own and enjoy may possess them for a few short years. But the teacher who lives on in hearts and homes made better by her quiet ministry will meet in the other world more than a few of her former pupils, who may never have thanked her here below. Meanwhile, let her commit to memory and often say to herself the collect written by John Henry Newman:

" O Lord, support us all the day long of this troublous life, until the shadows lengthen and the evening comes, and the busy world is hushed, and the fever of life is over, and our work is done. Then of Thy mercy grant us a safe lodging, and a holy rest, and peace at the last; through Jesus Christ our Lord. Amen."

ALL SAINTS' DAY

Ps. 122; Eph. 3:14–21

THE COMMUNION OF SAINTS

*" I bow my knees unto the Father of our Lord
Jesus Christ, of whom the whole family in heaven
and earth is named." — Eph. 3:14, 15.*

ON ALL SAINTS' DAY, 1517, Martin Luther stood before All Saints' Church at Wittenberg. There on the door
he posted his Ninety-five Theses. To the historian that
day marked the beginning of the Reformation. To us
the choice of All Saints' Day and All Saints' Church sug-
gests a different train of thought. It concerns the saints.
What do we Christians understand by the words, " All
the saints "? What do we affirm whenever we say together the clause in the Apostles' Creed: " I believe
in . . . the communion of saints "?

The word " communion " signifies fellowship. That
in turn points to what the saints have in common. Who,
then, are the saints? They are " the saved." Twice in the
Apocalypse we hear about the prayers of " all the saints,"
while the incense keeps ascending from the golden altar.
If we wish to know the identity of the saints, we can
listen to Paul as the chief of the apostles. Not only does
he himself seem to us the noblest of them all; he likewise stands as our chief interpreter of the Christian faith.

In Paul's letter to the Ephesians his theme is Christ
and the Church. He stresses the Church as the temple
of the indwelling Christ. In the text before us now the
apostle is praying about those whom the creed calls
saints: " I bow my knees unto the Father of our Lord
Jesus Christ, of whom the whole family in heaven and

earth is named." Many of us would start with things human and then work up toward the divine. But the apostle puts first the family of the redeemed in glory, and then points our eyes toward the children of God on earth. Let us follow his example.

1. *The Communion of Saints in Glory.* As Christians we praise God for the communion of saints in glory. In a certain hymnal fifteen songs are listed under the heading, " Communion of Saints." Almost without exception those songs concern the saints in heaven. Since the editor was the late Louis F. Benson, foremost American student of hymnology, few of us will question his interpretation of the words, " The Communion of Saints."

However, one element seems to be lacking in those songs. They leave the impression that the redeemed in glory are high and lifted up, far removed from their loved ones here on earth. In heaven with all its glory and peace the saints enjoy communion with one another and with the Lord Jesus. But can they likewise hold fellowship with us on earth, and we with them, through the Holy Spirit?

Here we enter a realm of mystery and wonder. The higher we ascend in thoughts about things heavenly the more we are likely to falter. Who among us feels at home in the rarity of the atmosphere, amid the splendor of the view? Nevertheless, without following the vagaries of certain extremists, we can be thankful for the testimony of many humble believers. They tell us of comfort and strength received through conscious communion with loved ones who have fallen asleep in Christ.

For an example turn to fiction. A current novel, *The Day Must Dawn,* by Agnes Sligh Turnbull, shows the hardships and perils of early pioneers on the frontier of western Pennsylvania. Toward the end of the story a woman of middle age lies down to die. Once a young girl with beauty and charm, she has grown old and haggard before her time. Listen as she whispers words of farewell to her only living child, a comely maiden now almost a woman:

" I'll never be far away from you. It's been like that with my own mother. A dozen times a day, like, it has always come to me. ' That's the way mother did,' or else, ' I can just hear mother say that! ' You never really lose your mother, my child, not when you love her. So don't you grieve! "

Now that William Lyon Phelps is with us no more in the flesh, some of us prize his words about Margaret Ogilvy, the mother of Sir James M. Barrie: " The spiritual presence of those whom we love is often more real than their physical existence. Especially is this true of the influence of parents on their offspring. They reach out from the grave invisible hands and guide our steps; their inaudible voices mould our opinions. We treat them with more deference than when they were here."

Once again the fellowship of kindred souls may be that of husband and wife. Who that reads the later poems of Robert Browning can question the reality and the beauty of his fellowship with the spirit of Elizabeth Barrett? In 1861 she went home to her God. Afterward for twenty-eight years her husband tarried on in the flesh. Far from seeming disconsolate, he continued to send out poems radiant with Christian hope and joy. In fact, the majority of his noblest writings appeared after she was with him no more, save as his constant inspiration. In the first volume published after her death he

gave out two of his most exquisite poems: *Prospice,* and
Rabbi Ben Ezra. The one sings directly about the life
beyond; the other, indirectly:

" My times be in Thy hand!
  Perfect the cup as planned!
Let age approve of youth, and death complete the same! "

The communion between heaven and earth may be
that of teacher and pupil. In South Carolina my most
thoughtful, elderly friends revered the memory of James
H. Thornwell. One of his most distinguished students
at the university testified that he had never faced a difficult problem or made a vital decision without having
been consciously guided and restrained by the spirit and
ideals of his most beloved professor. To what extent the
teacher in heaven could enjoy fellowship with his former
pupils still on earth, we mortals can never know. But we
rejoice to believe that the good the beloved have wrought
in us by their presence continues as an abiding influence
long after they have fallen asleep.

In fact, there is reason to think that we can hold fellowship, here on earth, with departed saints whom we
never have seen in the flesh. We who enter into the spirit
of the prophetic book of Hosea, or The First Epistle
General of Peter, can never escape the feeling that we
know the author better, and receive more from his fellowship, than from some good persons who live across
the street. The saints in glory dwell with the Lord Jesus,
in the home that is never far from the children of God
on earth. Whenever we come close to him, should we
not likewise feel near to them, as beloved friends of our
King?

All this and more appears to be wrapped up in the

words of the apostle about the family of the redeemed. Elsewhere in writing to the Corinthians he says, " Eye hath not seen, nor ear heard, neither have entered into the heart of man, the things which God hath prepared for them that love him." These glowing words tell of experiences that we ought to enjoy here on earth. Why then do we postpone to some future time the privilege of knowing and loving the saints of God in the unseen world? As we grow older in years the Lord grant that we may be richer in our friendships with his other children, who " through peril, toil and pain " have " climbed the steep ascent of heaven."

2. *The Communion of Saints Throughout the World Today*. Whenever we think of " the whole family in heaven and earth," we should give a large place to the Christian brethren across the Pacific. In December, 1938, the Madras Conference brought together representatives of all the Churches in the Far East, with a limited number of delegates from our western world. Instead of looking down on such " native Christians," many of us are learning to think of their leaders as second to none of the saints on earth.

For example, think of India's Bishop Azariah and Africa's James E. K. Aggrey; of Japan's Toyohiko Kagawa and China's C. T. Wong. In the years following World War II, we hope to enjoy more frequent interchanges of friendship between the newer Churches of the Far East and their older sisters here in the West. Meanwhile, we should remember that Christianity was born and cradled in the East, and that we may have far more to learn from our Oriental brethren than we are able to impart.

For the Body of Christ on earth the name in the

Apostles' Creed is "the Holy Catholic Church." Recently growing in favor is the title "the Ecumenical Church." A few decades ago many of us were talking much about "the evangelization of the world in this generation." Today we judge that the movement may have been marred by a certain degree of condescension, but surely the basic idea was Christian. Now we are learning to think of peoples in various lands as sons and daughters of our Heavenly Father. Hence we rejoice to welcome those other Christians as members in the redeemed family of which Christ is the Head.

All the while the chief obstacle to ecumenical fellowship springs out of race prejudice. When shall we Christians learn that God has "made of one every nation of men to dwell on all the face of the earth"? Since we expect to mingle with people of every race when we go home to God in heaven, why should we not enjoy more of such bliss here on earth?

In the forefront of the movement for the Ecumenical Church stand the missionaries. While we at home have been holding interracial conferences and discussing the obstacles to human brotherhood, our representatives throughout the Eastern world have been displaying the spirit of apostolic Christianity. As far back as 1886, James Chalmers, of New Guinea, wrote in his *Autobiography:* " On the first Sunday in December, I sat with a large number of Christian men and women and partook of the Lord's Supper, administered by a native pastor. There I was, shedding tears of joy, with men and women who as cannibals and savages only a few years before had sought our lives. What did it? It is the old story still of the Gospel of the cross."

Recently our sons in New Guinea have owed their

safety to the influence of such missionary martyrs as James Chalmers and Bishop John C. Patteson. But the fact that our boys had to sail over to the South Pacific, and there engage in war, affords a sad commentary on the status of the Ecumenical Church. A few decades ago we hoped that missions would do away with international strife. Now there is reason to believe that warfare has retarded the onward sweep of the ecumenical movement. Hence we should pray all the more fervently that God's Kingdom may come throughout the earth. Likewise should we raise here at home the seed corn for the extension of that Kingdom throughout every land for which the Saviour died.

3. *The Communion of Saints Here in the Home Church.* In the Apostles' Creed the words " the communion of saints " appear immediately before the phrase about the forgiveness of sins. Hence we infer that the saints are " the saved." Because the Heavenly Father has forgiven our sins, he has admitted us to the household of the redeemed. In the family group known as the local Church we as the people of God enjoy fellowship one with another, because we have much in common through our love for Jesus Christ.

Meanwhile, some of us need to revise our conceptions of the word " saint." We think of the term as applying to such a remote hero of the faith as Saint Francis, or such a heroine as Saint Teresa. Surely the term ought to embrace both of them, and various other worthies in the Roman Church. But are there no saints among Protestants now? Have we none at all in our home Church? Why should we not think of our godliest elders and deacons as Saint William and Saint George, and of our most pious women as Saint Margaret and Saint Catherine? Why do we assume that all the saints have dwelt far away and long ago? Must we wait until our Christian brothers and sisters have gone home to God before we discover that we have been holding communion with some of his choicest saints?

When the Apostle Paul wrote about " the whole family in heaven and earth " he meant to include his friends in many a local Church. In writing to the congregation at Corinth, at Rome, or at Philippi, he addressed the brethren as those "called to be saints." In the epistle before us now he wrote to " the saints which are at Ephesus." If the letter went from Church to Church, as many scholars suppose, the official who read the message aloud would substitute the name of his own city. For instance, he would speak " to the saints that are at Thessalonica," or else " Berea." Then he would deliver orally what we call the Epistle to the Ephesians. In other words, the apostle thought of Church members as " called to be saints." The saints are the saved.

My friend, as a part of the Christian Church, you belong to the mightiest throng in all God's universe. Not only does the fellowship of the saints include those now assembled in the sanctuary, but all the other children of God scattered abroad over the world today. The larger number of the redeemed have passed beyond the veil that men call death. In that other home, which never should seem far from God's children on earth, the saints are beckoning to us now. They assure us that though the way on earth seem long, and the going often hard, the grace of our God is more than sufficient for each of his children. In the life beyond he will crown all that he has begun in the saints here on earth.

Wherefore, like the apostle, make these words your own: " I bow my knees unto the Father of our Lord Jesus Christ, of whom the whole family in heaven and earth is named." Thank God that as a Christian you can enter into the communion of saints!

SOLDIER'S DAY

Ps. 27; Heb. 11:32 to 12:4

THE CHRISTIAN CONQUEST OF FEAR

*" The Lord is my light and my salvation; whom
shall I fear? the Lord is the strength of my life; of
whom shall I be afraid? " — Ps. 27:1.*

THESE words come from a soldier. He appears to be
young, at least in heart. His song concerns the faith of a
fearless warrior. Doubtless he thinks of fear as the
mightiest emotion of the human soul. At least fear
seems to be more potent than aught save love, for " perfect love casteth out fear." In the world of affairs fear
causes panics, brings on depression, and leads to war. In
the soul of many a man today fear leads to despondency,
uncertainty, and helplessness. If his heart is not right
with God, or if his mind is distraught, fear may lead him
to self-murder.

The occasions of fear are so well known that they need
not detain us now. Some of them relate to sickness and
accident; others, to work and its reward; others again,
to the unknown future. Add to the list as many occasions
of fear as you wish. You will find that some are real but
that most are imaginary. Beneath them all you may discover the fact of sin. For the sake of simplicity, however,
let us consider the occasions of fear in the heart of a
warrior who is striving earnestly to do the will of God.

The occasions of fear seem to be countless; the cause
proves to be unexpectedly simple. In the heart of a man
who wants to be righteous, the cause of fear must be
lack of faith. If you could gather all the occasions of
fear and load them onto a truck, so as to dump them

out on the rubbish heap, on that truck you might put the sign: " Human Fears, Caused by Lack of Faith." The remedy for all kinds of unworthy fear, therefore, must be old-fashioned faith. What, then, do we understand by faith? It means human weakness laying hold on divine power, to supply all a man's needs. More simply, faith means trusting God.

For what should a man look to God in faith? The answer depends on what he needs at the moment. Ofttimes the need has to do with fear. In the case before us a warrior sings about three ways in which religion deals with the fears of a godly soldier on the field of battle. These same truths apply to everyone in the house of the Lord today. Is not each one of us engaged in a conflict where faith ought to triumph over fear? " This is the victory that overcometh the world, even our faith." Remember that faith means trusting God. Trusting him for what?

1. *Faith Means Trusting God for Guidance.* " The Lord is my light." In the Scriptures, as in the hymnal, light often serves as a symbol of guidance from above. Like Moses, in days of peril long ago, the man of faith endures " as seeing him who is invisible." Perhaps it would be more correct to speak of such guidance as coming from within, much as the Friends tarry for the leading of " the inner light." Still another name for such an attitude of trust would be seeing faith.

> " Lead, kindly Light, amid th' encircling gloom,
> Lead Thou me on."

As a rule guidance comes gradually. Literally, this word means " step by step."

" I do not ask to see
The distant scene — one step enough for me."

In June, 1833, when John Henry Newman wrote
"Lead, Kindly Light," he was beginning to recover
from a critical illness. Perhaps for that reason he
was battling with all sorts of fears about his unknown
future. Since he was only thirty-two years of age, and was
expecting to live rather than die, his song ought to help
many a man who needs to trust in God for daily
guidance. During that month of June, when young Newman was becalmed out on the Mediterranean, he learned
to look upon life as a voyage and upon religion as trusting the Lord for guidance. Of late many of us have been
thinking about life as a battlefield. Even so, faith means
turning to God for guidance.

" Thrice blest is he to whom is given
The instinct which can tell
That God is on the field when He
Is most invisible."

2. *Faith Also Means Trusting God for Deliverance.*
Every man needs saving faith as well as seeing faith.
" The Lord is my light, and my salvation." That blessed
old word " salvation " literally means " deliverance."
Through faith the Lord God sets a man free. Free from
what? From whatever evils beset his soul and prevent
him from fighting the good fight of faith. Usually we
think of salvation as deliverance from gross outward
sins, such as drunkenness, gambling, and adultery, all of
which may team up together. Those excesses are real,
but the psalmist is singing about deliverance from perils
far less visible.

What, then, are the evils that sometimes possess a
good man's soul? Near the top of the list stand worry,

despondency, and fear — notably fear. Of what avail is
a man's religion if it does not set him free from these
moods that often threaten to overwhelm his soul? Because of such conditions within, the Bible abounds in
golden texts concerning deliverance from the foes of the
soul. The most beloved of all the psalms, for instance,
shows how a young warrior sits down to eat in the very
face of death: " Thou preparest a table before me in the
presence of mine enemies."

God promises to deliver a believing man from fear,
but not from danger. This truth shines out from the
record about Daniel in the den of lions. In the palace
one night the king could not sleep. Early in the morning
he arose from the royal bed and hastened to the lions'
den. There he cried out to his friend within: " O Daniel,
servant of the living God, is thy God, whom thou serv-
est continually, able to deliver thee from the lions? " At
once came the reply, in substance: " My God is able! "
The extent of a man's deliverance from fear depends on
the degree of his faith. How is it with you, my friend? Is
your God able?

Someone may be thinking that David and Daniel lived
long ago, in a day when life was simple and faith was
normal. Sometimes we exaggerate the naturalness and
the ease of trusting God in the olden times. At any rate
the Lord is able to deliver any man from his fears today.
For instance, the late William Oxley Thompson,
president of Ohio State University, earned the reputa-
tion of being able to do more work and better work than
any other man in his part of the country. His young
pastor once inquired about the secret of such ability to
toil without inner friction. The schoolman smiled as he
explained, " My religion taught me long ago to live with-

out worry, to work without hurry, and to look forward without fear."

3. *Faith Likewise Means Trusting God for Victory.* " The Lord is the strength of my life; of whom shall I be afraid? " Conquest of a man's fears ought to mean far more than guidance, or even deliverance. When a man receives guidance, the occasions of fear remain. At any moment he may be compelled to cry out again for God's leading. Even when he has been delivered from his fears, they are likely to come back on the morrow, or else to-day, reinforced and doubly strong. Surely God never intended that one of his children should forever be enslaved by fears.

When by faith a man conquers these foes, they should become his servants. In the days when our fathers landed at Jamestown or Plymouth Rock, they dreaded the forces of nature, such as electricity and fire. But in these later times men have conquered most of those natural forces, and have put them under harness. In the automobile and the airplane, for instance, many of those powers work together to wipe out the limits of time and space. A few years ago much of the energy produced by the automobile engine was wasted. But now a good deal of that surplus power is harnessed and set to work in starting the motor, keeping it going, affording illumination at night, and producing heat during the winter.

Do you suppose that the Almighty, who has given us men the ability to harness the forces of nature, wishes any one of us to subsist as a slave to fear? No, if a man's faith in God is practical, it will supply the power to conquer his fears. Without such ability to control his inner being, a man might become almost as useless as an auto-

mobile without a storage battery. When a man has sub-
dued the mighty forces within his soul, and has put them
to work in doing the will of God, such a master of himself ought to sing with the old-time warrior: " The Lord
is the strength of my life; of whom shall I be afraid? "

How then can one change fear from a liability into an
asset? The text shows that the transformation comes
partly through worship. In every case before us this
morning the man in view has learned how to triumph
over fear by lifting up his heart to God. Sometimes with
the multitude who keep holy day, more often in private
as he meditates on God, any man who trusts in the Lord
can rise into an atmosphere of greater visibility. There
by faith he can look upon life as it is in the eyes of the
Father. By adoring him, therefore, one can use aright
all the powers that might otherwise be worse than
wasted through that sort of inner friction known as fear.

Even when one must be far from home and Church,
in peril by land or sea, the memory of some hour in the
sanctuary may bring the strength to conquer rising fears.
During World War I, a young kinsman of President
Woodrow Wilson served as a driver of an ambulance
truck. With him up front sat another youth, so that if one
were killed the other could keep the car in use. On a
certain night shot and shell were falling on every side.
As the two were drawing near to the front-line trenches,
with no lights on the truck, the young soldier in view
began to fear that he might grow afraid. Then he started
humming to himself the melody of the anthem that he
had learned in the Chapel Choir at Princeton University: " The Lord is my light and my salvation; whom
shall I fear? the Lord is the strength of my life; of whom
shall I be afraid? "

Soon the young man forgot about himself and his

fears. That night he performed his duty; the next day he was decorated for bravery. His experience on the field of battle reminds us that one of God's appointed ways for conquering fear is the doing of the work in hand, especially if duty calls for helping those in need. From this point of view try a simple experiment: The next time you feel that fears are about to get the better of your faith, seek out some person in distress and use your God-given powers in being a Good Samaritan. At last, weary in body and ready for food and sleep, you will find that your fears have vanished like street shadows in the light of the home fireside. In brief, the Lord can always find something for a fearful saint to do.

The faith that conquers fear calls for hope in God. On the field of battle the soldier is aware that the passing moment may be his last on earth. He feels certain that the cause for which he fights is just, and that some day righteousness will prevail. Hence he should be ready to lay down his life. If he felt sure that the forces of anti-God would win the decisive battle, and then impose a shameful peace, how could he keep from fear? Since he looks forward to using in the unseen world the powers developed here, why should he dread the adventure of " going west "? But if he thought that this life was all, how could he face the future unafraid?

The faith that triumphs over fear must come from God. In the midst of perils and alarms, he is waiting to guide you every one. In the face of pitfalls known and unknown, he has promised to deliver you from every fear. But he does not offer respite from peril; you will never be free from danger until you are dead. Best of all, he stands ready to impart strength and wisdom to master all your fears. Then you can put them to work in doing his will. By his grace you may become like John

Knox, of whom it used to be said, " He fears God so much that he does not dread the face of any mortal man." He did not even cringe before the ire of a strong-willed woman!

My friend, why not learn our text by heart? Why not form the habit of repeating it again and again? In the midst of the darkness, if you awake out of a night-mare, and feel the sweat streaming from your brow, re-peat this old-time creed of a godly warrior. On the eve of battle, when it seems that your little world has come to its end, whisper softly to yourself this ancient hymn of trust and hope. On a man-of-war, if the ship threatens to sink with all on board, remember that you will go down into the hands of God. Those hands are strong, and his heart is kind. " The Lord is the strength of my life; of whom shall I be afraid? "

Doubtless someone is asking: " Why bring such thoughts into the sanctuary? Why not let us worship God in peace? " Alas, my friend, how can you talk of peace in a world where there is no peace? Here in God's house the storms may not be raging. Nevertheless, while the sun is shining and the south wind is blowing softly, make ready for the storm that is sure to arise. In the quietness of the sanctuary commit yourself into the hands of God. Turn to him now, so that " when the snows begin, and the blasts denote " you are " nearing the place, the power of the night, the press of the storm," still you can sing with the warrior of old:

> " The Lord is my light and my salvation;
>   Whom shall I fear?
> The Lord is the strength of my life;
>   Of whom shall I be afraid? "

THANKSGIVING TIME
Ps. 107:23–32; Phil. 4:1–13

THE GIVING OF THANKS IN A STORM
" They cry unto the Lord in their trouble,
And he bringeth them out of their distresses.

. . . .

" Oh that men would praise the Lord for his
goodness,
And for his wonderful works to the children of
men! " — Ps. 107:28, 31.

" HOW can we give thanks to God in these dark and awful days? " Again and again the query comes from men and women who pray. At times there may be a lull in the tumult out on the expanse known as life. But in the past decade storm has succeeded storm, and the worst may be yet to come. If so, the winds will lift up the waves of the deep, until they seem mountain-high. Hence there comes the question, How can men and women pray and give thanks to God when the storm is on the deep and the ship seems destined to go down with all on board?

For light amid such darkness turn to the One Hundred and Seventh Psalm. In the *Spectator* Joseph Addison declares that this poem affords our loftiest word picture of a ship in the grasp of a storm. In his essay, " The Mighty Force of Ocean's Troubled Flood," Addison says, " Of all the objects I have ever seen, none affects my imagination so much as the ocean." He tells us that he cannot look upon the calmest sea without a " pleasing astonishment," and that when the waters are worked up into a tempest, so that the horizon on every side appears to be full of foaming billows and floating mountains, he cannot describe the " agreeable horror " that springs from such a display of titanic forces let loose for destruction.

So let us turn to the psalm and to the subject, The Giving of Thanks in a Storm.

1. *In a Time of Storm Men Ought to Discover God.* Listen again to Addison. He is speaking as a believer in the Most High God: " It is impossible for me to survey this world of fluid matter without thinking on the Hand that poured it out." He says that often he has been aboard a wooden ship tossed in a tempest, and that every time the experience has proved a means of grace. Although the Lord God never leaves us alone, whether by sea or land, he seldom seems so near and so mighty as when a ship out on the deep struggles and shudders in the grasp of a tornado.

Especially at Thanksgiving time, when the world has been at war, we mortals should think of a storm with reference to God. When the sun keeps shining out over the sea, and the south wind blowing softly, we may become concerned about many things else and forget all about God. Hence the late Baron Von Hügel affirmed, " It is harder for a healthy person to be really religious " than for one whose body is " a constant failure." However cowardly the course may seem, a man is far more likely to discover God when no one else can deliver than when everything seems to be right with the world. In recent years, alas, our whole earth has been sick nigh unto death. Why not " try God "?

Sometimes we ask why he permits storms to arise at sea, or even within the soul. The entire matter must remain a mystery. Still we surmise that he must employ drastic means to make us know that we are frail, and that we cannot have peace at heart unless we trust in the Lord. In the words of the psalm before us now, strong men discover him when at sea on a vessel driven by the wind and tossed, so that even the sailors reel to and fro, staggering like men drunk, and are at their wits' end.

Similar testimony hails from one of the ablest thinkers of our time, P. A. Sorokin, of Harvard. For a score of years he has been an involuntary exile from Russia, the land of his birth. His recent volume bears the title, *Man and Society in Calamity*. After a discussion of crises in our world, both of yesterday and today, this wise observer declares: " The principal steps in the progress of mankind toward a spiritual religion and a noble code of ethics have been taken under the impact of great catastrophes. The periods of comparative stability, order, and mutual well-being have scarcely ever given rise to a truly great religion. . . . A rough estimate indicates that from seventy to eighty-five per cent of all eminent social thinkers have suffered ostracism, imprisonment, banishment, or have become voluntary exiles from their homeland. . . . Herein lies perhaps the justification for the tragedies of civilization."

Whatever the reason, in time of storm countless men have discovered God. In recent days of peril many a warrior has found him in the Bible. In December, 1936, when General Chiang Kai-shek was kidnaped and held captive for days, he requested nothing save a copy of the Scriptures. There he found God as never before. Strange to tell, the captive was released, unharmed, on Christmas Day. In November, 1942, when Captain Eddie Rickenbacker and his seven comrades were cast adrift on a boundless sea, they too discovered God as he makes him-

self known through the Book. Much the same experience
has come to hosts of young men who serve in the ranks.
Their names are written in heaven, where the portals
of late must have been thronged with unknown soldiers.
Is it any wonder that we can sing about the life everlasting in terms of triumph?

> " Ten thousand times ten thousand
>   In sparkling raiment bright,
> The armies of the ransomed saints
>   Throng up the steeps of light;
> 'Tis finished, all is finished,
>   Their fight with death and sin:
> Fling open wide the golden gates,
>   And let the victors in."

2. *In a Time of Storm Men Should Learn to Pray.*
Here again, the soul of a man differs from a machine.
While one person prays, others may curse. Many who
cry out to God for deliverance from the storm appear to
forget him as soon as the winds subside. Nevertheless,
as every lover of biography has learned, the men and
the women who pray best are those who have suffered
most. In London at the City Temple, which now lies in
ruins, Joseph Parker used to declare that every pew contained at least one broken heart. Likewise did he insist
that " prosperity cannot read the Twenty-third Psalm ":
" Yea, though I walk through the valley of the shadow
of death, I will fear no evil: for thou art with me; thy
rod and thy staff they comfort me."

For what does one pray in a time of storm? Ofttimes
one cries out in a confession of sin. When Isaiah's heart
felt heavy because his king lay dead, the young man saw
a vision of the Holy God. At once the worshiper exclaimed: " Woe is me! for I am undone; because I am a

man of unclean lips, and I dwell in the midst of a people of unclean lips: for mine eyes have seen the King." Never do our sins appear more ghastly than when we look on them in the light that streams from the throne of God.

In the bleakest month of 1917, President Woodrow Wilson called for a nationwide " Hour of Prayer." At noon on a certain day in the midst of the week throngs of God-fearing folk assembled in various places of worship. In our own Church at Columbia, South Carolina, we joined in confession of our sins and in pleas for God's mercy. With many of us that hour of supplication lives in memory as an experience on the mountaintop. As citizens of a land engaged in war we confessed the wrongdoings of our hearts and of our beloved land. Then we cast ourselves and our all upon the mercy of God. Would that today as a people we might fall on our faces before the One against whom we have sinned times without number! Then we should exclaim: " O Lord, revive thy work in the midst of the years, in the midst of the years make known; in wrath remember mercy."

During an hour of peril God's people may implore him to deliver. In the One Hundred and Seventh Psalm the refrain rings out four times: " Then they cry unto the Lord in their trouble, and he saveth them out of their distresses." Without becoming selfish, such prayers may be quite personal. When one is engaged in work for the Kingdom of God, why not ask him for time to complete the task assigned? Here again, turn to biography. Take Mary Slessor of Calabar. How could that lone woman keep calm amid the perils of darkest Africa, and thus become a power for the uplift of the Dark Continent? Listen to her simple explanation:

" My life is one long, daily, hourly record of answered

prayer. For physical health, for mental overstrain, for guidance marvelously given, for errors and dangers averted, for food provided at the exact hour needed, for everything that goes to make up life and my poor service, I can testify with wonder-stricken awe that God answers prayer."

3. *In a Time of Storm Men Should Give Thanks to God.* In the psalm before us now another refrain rings out four times: " Oh that men would praise the Lord for his goodness, and for his wonderful works to the children of men! " First the cry for deliverance and then the song of thanksgiving! In all the worship of the Old Testament two notes prevail: The one is prayer for the pardon of sins; the other is gratitude for God's mercies. From our modern point of view the Children of Israel endured an endless succession of hard times, with many a calamity. Nevertheless, their leaders called for songs of gratitude and praise to God. Largely for this reason at the Thanksgiving service every year both the Scripture lesson and the text of the hour are chosen from The Book of Psalms. " O give thanks unto the Lord, . . . for his mercy endureth for ever."

In time of storm the ship may breast the waves and bring everyone safe to land. If so, they should render thanks to God. For example, think of Alexander Duff, one of the most brilliant sons of the Scottish Church. In February, 1830, he and his young bride were slowly sailing out to India, there to begin a lifework for God. As they drew near to the Cape of Good Hope the ship ran aground, and erelong was beaten to pieces by the waves. Providentially, the passengers and the sailors " escaped all safe to land."

On the shore one of the seamen picked up a package, in which he found a Bible and a Scottish Psalmbook. Each of them bore the name of Alexander Duff. Because of that shipwreck the young missionary lost his library of eight hundred books, carefully chosen, for he was a scholar. On that day he determined henceforth to be a man of one Book. He knew many others, but he trusted in one. Gathering about him the other survivors from the wreck, he read the One Hundred and Seventh Psalm. Then he offered a prayer of thanksgiving. " Oh that men would praise the Lord for his goodness, and for his wonderful works to the children of men! "

" But what if the ship goes down with all on board? " Even so, believers in Christ should trust in God, and give him thanks. Surely they know that underneath the children of the Heavenly Father are the everlasting arms. When a man-made ship goes down into the deep, the saints are secure in the hands that were pierced. What else do we profess whenever we stand up to say the closing words of the Apostles' Creed? " I believe in . . . the forgiveness of sins; the resurrection of the body; and the life everlasting." These triumphant affirmations find an echo in the song by the Scottish-American poet-preacher, the late Robert Freeman:

> " When souls go down to the sea by ship,
> And the dark ship's name is Death,
> Why mourn and wail at the vanishing sail?
> Though outward bound, God's world is round,
> And only a ship is Death.
>
> " When I go down to the sea by ship,
> And Death unfurls her sail,
> Weep not for me, for there will be
> A living host on another coast
> To beckon and cry, ' All hail! ' "

BIBLE SUNDAY
Isa. 55; II Tim. 3:14–17

THE BIBLE AS ONE WORLD
" God, who at sundry times and in divers manners spake in time past . . . by the prophets, hath in these last days spoken by his son." — Heb. 1:1, 2a.

THESE familiar words tell about the Bible as a whole. Many signs point to a rediscovery of the Scriptures. Men and women appear to be reading the Book more largely today than at any time in recent years. Better still, some of them insist on looking at the Scriptures with open eyes. Among other questions, these friends keep asking: " Is the Bible a single work? Did Sir Walter Scott speak aright when he asked his son-in-law to bring the Book? " " What book? " said the younger man. " The Bible! " was the answer. " There is but one! "

Certain scholars have been teaching that the Scriptures form a " divine library." Of course that is true. The phrase seems to have come from Saint Jerome, who died in 420 A.D. A similar title, " The Books," hails from his contemporary, Saint Chrysostom, " the golden-mouthed preacher." Well did those worthies know that the " divine library " consists of sixty-six books. In terms of geography, they represent as many varieties of climate, population, and soil as the physical world where we mortals dwell. Nevertheless, we can think of the Bible in terms of the recent best seller, written by Wendell Willkie, and entitled *One World.*

One world! According to men of science, the physical world is one. However it came to its present form, our earth moves as a single unit. The same ought to be true of all nations. God has made them to be one. In like fashion, according to the saints, there stands the fact of Biblical oneness. In terms of geography, the Scriptural world comprises two hemispheres. The larger one, with the longer history, we call the Old Testament. The smaller one, which we love still more, we know as the New. All the while we ought to think of the two hemispheres as " One World." Together they constitute a single Book of revealed truth and duty, under the name of the Holy Scriptures.

One world! Doubtless we are making the truth appear unduly simple. At all events, we can give thanks for each hemisphere of the Biblical world. The Old Testament is good, because it reveals much about God. The New is better, for it tells more about God in Christ. Without the Old Testament, as the source book of Biblical history, we could scarcely comprehend the New, as the completion of the inspired record. From this point of view the two main parts are bound together by their relation to Jesus Christ.

One world, in two hemispheres! The Old Testament shows how God prepared for the advent of the Saviour. The New reveals how the Spirit made known the coming of Christ. If we are to understand the New Testament, therefore, we must start with the Old. According to Saint Augustine, " The New is in the Old concealed; the Old is in the New revealed." All the while we should look upon the two hemispheres as inseparable halves of God's " one world." Such is the " latest " message from the throne, for through the Bible God is speaking now.

1. *The Old Testament Reveals Much About God.* In our text the apostle writes about him as speaking

through the prophets. These words point to the authors of the Old Testament. In this use of the term, " the prophets " included all the holy men of old who spake and wrote for God. The phrase, " At sundry times and in divers manners," refers to the variety of their books. Unlike the New Testament, which appears to have been written within less than three generations, the Old seems to have stretched out over almost a thousand years. Whereas the New consists largely of narratives and epistles in prose, the Old includes a wealth of inspiring verse. As literature, both in variety and in splendor, the Old surpasses the New. Nevertheless, when bound together, the Old and the New form " one world," full of revealed truth and duty. Here, then, we should discover divine power for human needs.

In the Old Testament God makes himself known through all sorts of men and in countless ways. As a rule he reveals himself indirectly. Sometimes he even appears to be hiding himself. The Book of Esther, for instance, contains no mention of his name and no allusion to his being. Even so, God is standing " within the shadow keeping watch above His own." From time to time he makes bare his mighty arm. More often he speaks through holy men who know him well. Through these same heralds of righteousness and hope God is speaking to us now: " To day, if ye will hear his voice, harden not your hearts."

This larger hemisphere of our " one world " consists of three grand divisions. For convenience we shall follow the arrangement of the books in our English versions. The order of the parts is somewhat different in the Hebrew Bible. However, that also consists of three grand divisions. For want of better names we usually speak of

them as "books of history," "books of poetry," and
"books of prophecy." Of course such terms are "popular" rather than scholarly. What matters most is the
light that the various parts of the Old Testament throw
on the meaning of God in human experience today.

The "books of history" reach from Genesis through
Esther. In form they largely consist of "well told stories
taken from life." In substance they show much about
the God who makes himself known in action. The book
of Genesis reveals him at work in a patriarchal household. Exodus concerns the deliverance of the chosen
nation. Leviticus has to do with the worship of the Hebrew Church. Thus we might go on, through book after
book, to see in "broken lights" many a truth about God
in his dealings with men like ourselves. The Book of
Joshua, for instance, relates to conquest, whereas The
Book of Judges reports disintegration because men forgot about God. The twin books of Samuel tell how God
guided and restrained his children during a period of
national reconstruction.

Before we turn from these books of historical narrative
we ought to face a difficult problem. It concerns the
spiritual values of Old Testament history. When that
eloquent unbeliever Robert G. Ingersoll used to wax
fervent about "the mistakes of Moses," the attack cen-
tered on the books now before us. Ingersoll may not
have known that they were written to tell about God,
rather than Moses. Even so, if the skeptic had been better
informed about the Bible, he might have shifted his
attack to the moral standards of Old Testament history.
For instance, when a young man reads the closing chap-
ters of The Book of Judges he may exclaim: "Why do
you bind these records in the same book with the Sermon

on the Mount? In the realm of morals is the Bible all one world? "

In response to such inquiries from our young people, let us frankly admit that Old Testament history raises serious problems about ethics. Some of them we cannot solve. Looking upon this part of the Old Testament in the large, however, we find comparatively few pages black with the slime of unspeakable sin, or reeking with the gore of God's suffering saints. Wherever such records appear, they should prove " profitable for . . . correction." Do they not show our human nature " red in tooth and claw "? These parts of the Book provide a mirror, in which we mortals can see ourselves as we really are, without God's redeeming grace. In view of what has recently occurred on the battlefields of China and of Poland, is there no need for such a mirror now? Has human nature changed since the days of the Judges?

When we move over into the " books of poetry " we find ourselves in a more beautiful grand division of our " one world." These writings, some of which appear as prose, tell how the Lord God makes himself known to the heart. The Book of Job deals with the agelong problem: Why must a good man suffer? or else with the possibility of disinterested goodness. The Book of Psalms presents beautiful hymns of praise, songs of prayer, and poems of teaching. The Proverbs contains exalted poetry, with less sublime ethical teachings, all showing how a young man should live in the busy world of affairs. Ecclesiastes, a book full of exquisite prose, guides us in weighing all things good, only to find that the *summum bonum* is the religion of the heart. The Song of Solomon consists of beautiful lyric poems about " the way of a man with a maid."

Amid all this truth and splendor the reader longs for still more light from above. Hence he should turn to the " books of the prophets." Here he will find himself in the mountain country of the Old Testament. For a while he may feel lost. He will never find the going easy, but if he perseveres he will learn how to follow the leading of such holy men as Isaiah and Jeremiah, Hosea and Amos. In time the reader of the prophetic books may learn even more about God than from the other grand divisions of the Old Testament.

The prophets were God's chosen interpreters. Usually they spoke about the Kingdom, as it concerned men and nations of that olden time. But ever and anon one of the seers would lift up his eyes to the hills and behold the signs of the coming Redeemer. As a rule the stress fell on his work as the Ideal King. At other times the prophetic word had to do with the Suffering Servant, whom we know as the Christ of the cross. Is it any wonder that many of us regard the prophetic books as the Old Testament's nearest approach to the spirit of the New? Do they not encourage us to think of the Bible as " one world "?

When we glance back over the Old Testament, therefore, let us thank God for its variety, and for its " one increasing purpose." Now that we have looked at the three grand divisions, still we feel a sense of incompleteness. Even if we were not familiar with the facts about the New Testament, we should expect some sort of sequel to the Old, and that on a distinctly higher level. In other words, we should long to discover a new world, where we could come still closer to the heart of God. But before we turn to this newer hemisphere let us remind ourselves that it also belongs to our " one world."

When our fathers and mothers sailed over the Atlantic in quest of the New, they still kept in touch with the Old.

The Old is good, but the New is better. Much the same principle applies in other realms. For example, think of a church building. In a certain parish, owing to the size and shape of the downtown lot, the architect planned for an edifice with two main divisions. Since the people could not afford to erect it all at once, at first the builders provided only the ground floor. Within those spacious quarters the people loved to assemble for worship, for Bible study, and for social enjoyment. All the time they worked and prayed for the privilege of completing their beloved church. In later years, now that the new has been built upon the old, they continue to use all of those rooms on the ground floor. But they feel much more at home in the sanctuary upstairs. That is where they come closest to the God who reveals himself supremely in Christ and his cross.

2. *The New Testament Reveals More About God in Christ.* " God, who at sundry times and in divers manners spake in times past . . . by the prophets, hath in these last days spoken by his Son." In him the edifice of divine revelation became complete. If we revert to our former figure we can think of the new hemisphere as comprising three grand divisions, unequal in size. They too constitute major parts of our " one world."

The first five books of the New Testament state the facts about Jesus Christ. On these facts we base our belief in him as Redeemer and Lord. The Gospel According to Saint Matthew stresses his teachings, which concern the Kingdom. Saint Mark presents the Lord Jesus as the " Strong Son of God." His Gospel of service shows the life and work of Christ. Saint Luke tells about the ideal personality of him who is " Fairest Lord Jesus." Here is the Gospel of grace, as well as of prayer. The Fourth Gospel differs widely from the other three, for Saint John stresses the Deity of our Saviour. The Acts of the Apostles shows the power of the risen Lord. Through the Holy Spirit the living Christ builds up the Kingdom of God.

These first five books of the New Testament make known the facts about Jesus Christ. The Epistles afford an interpretation of the facts. These letters tell us little of what Jesus said and did. Rather do they show who he is and what difference his coming ought to make in our hearts and lives, as well as throughout the world. Is it any wonder, then, that more than a few of the saints look upon the Epistles, especially those of Paul and John, as the most helpful portion of the Bible?

Even so, our " one world " cannot yet be complete. Somewhat by itself stands The Revelation of Saint John the Divine. According to James Denney, master theologian of yesterday, the Apocalypse is " the most Christian book in the Bible." Some of us may not share that lofty estimate. The reason may be that we have not yet learned to appreciate this crowning part of the New Testament. Denney means that the book of Revelation tells most of all about Christ as the Lord of Glory. In terms of mystery and wonder the Apocalypse bids us look forward to the consummation of the ages. Instead of making us fearful that every day and in every way the world must grow worse and worse, until it will end in eternal night,

the book of Revelation bids us rest secure in the promise
that Christ shall rule over earth and heaven as King of
Kings and Lord of Lords.

Thus we have looked at the Bible as all " one world."
We find the Old Testament good because it tells about
God in his dealings with men like ourselves. We love
the New Testament more because it reveals God in
Christ as our Saviour and King. All the while we have
taken for granted that some portions of the Book ought
to be more precious than others. According to saintly
Richard Baxter, " The Scripture is like a man's body,
where some parts are for the preservation of the rest, and
may be maimed without death (to the whole) . The sense
is the soul of Scripture; the letter is but the body or the
vehicle." Nevertheless, the written Word of God, like
the human body, is all " one world."

As a witness to the power of the Book as a whole, give
heed to Woodrow Wilson: " The opinion of the Bible
bred in me, not only by the teaching of my home when
I was a boy, but also by every turn and experience of my
life, and every step of study, is that it constitutes the
supreme source of revelation, the revelation of the meaning of life, the nature of God, and the spiritual needs of
men. It is the only guide of life which really leads the
spirit in the way of peace and salvation. If men could
but be made to know it, intimately and for what it really
is, we should have secured both individual and social
regeneration." Through this Book, therefore, the peoples of earth can find what Woodrow Wilson in his closing days termed " The Road Away from Revolution."

Wherein lies the secret of such transforming power?
If we could ask the books of the Bible, they would join
in a mighty chorus: " The Hand that made us is

divine! " In doing so God employed all sorts of human beings, each in a fashion all his own. Even so, the Lord must have guided and restrained those men of old, for often they wrote more wisely than they knew. Through the Church he has kept the Book until the present hour. By his Holy Spirit, God is waiting to lead us into an understanding of the Bible. He has promised that the knowledge of the truth shall make us free. If we would see a nation and a world " pure and free," let us " make our own spirits pure and free by this baptism of the Holy Scriptures."

Through this Book, God is speaking to our hearts and minds. When we hear his voice we know that it comes from him. These are truths of Christian experience. They " need no guarantee beyond themselves." " If I am asked why I receive Scripture as the Word of God, and as the only perfect rule of faith and life, I answer with all the fathers of the Protestant Church: Because the Bible is the only record of the redeeming love of God, because in the Bible alone I find God drawing near to man in Christ Jesus, and declaring to us in him the divine will for our salvation. This record I know to be true by the witness of His Spirit in my heart, whereby I am assured that none other than God Himself is able to speak such words to my soul."

That is a modern interpretation of our text: " God, who at sundry times and in divers manners spake in time past unto the fathers by the prophets, hath in these last days spoken unto us by his Son." What a message for Bible Sunday! From this hour onward may you see in the Book God's " one world." As you know it better you will love it more. You will find added joy in teaching the Bible to your children, and your children's children yet unborn. When at last God calls you to his other home, you will thank him there for the way he has spoken through the Bible, and supremely in his Son. Let us pray:

" Blessed Lord, who hast caused all holy Scripture to be written for our learning; Grant that we may in such wise hear them, read, mark, learn, and inwardly digest them, that by patience and comfort of thy holy Word, we may embrace, and ever hold fast, the blessed hope of everlasting life, which thou hast given us in our Saviour Jesus Christ. Amen."

" The God of peace, that brought again from the dead our Lord Jesus, that great shepherd of the sheep, through the blood of the everlasting covenant, make you perfect in every good work to do his will, working in you that which is well-pleasing in his sight, through Jesus Christ; to whom be glory for ever and ever. Amen."